COLLECTED WORKS OF
GUSTAV STICKLEY

Edited by
Stephen Gray and Robert Edwards

Published by
TURN of the CENTURY EDITIONS

Six Varick Street
New York, N.Y. 10013

CONTENTS

"*Cabinet Work from the Craftsman Workshops*" provided by James and Janeen Marrin
"*What is Wrought in the Craftsman Workshops*" provided by Albert Albano
"*Things Wrought*" by the United Crafts provided by Eric Silver.

INTRODUCTION

History is always more fiction than fact. The greater the span of time between the historian and his subject, the greater the loss of factual evidence and the greater the imagination required to reweave the broken threads. The Arts and Crafts Movement reached the apex of it's influence on American society just 75 years ago yet the number of people who can give us firsthand information has dwindled severely. Our belated interest is, for the most part, already dependent on the writings of the Movement's leading exponents.

Fortunately there remains a wealth of such primary material to help us reconstruct this complex period. During the intervening years, libraries have not dealt kindly with these invaluable sources and most are now harbored in inaccessible private collections. Gustav Stickley was a prolific writer but only recently has his own interpretation of the Movement been readily available.

This collection of Stickley's writings and catalogues should serve not only to preserve a clear perception of his work but also to continue, as he intended, to be a guide to the Arts and Craftsman's utopian concept of art as a stimulus to life.

Robert L. Edwards
November, 1981

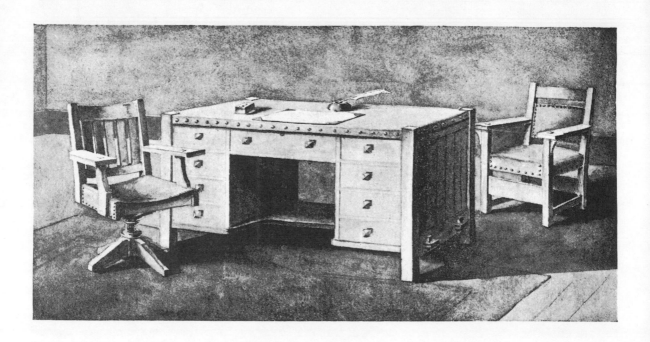

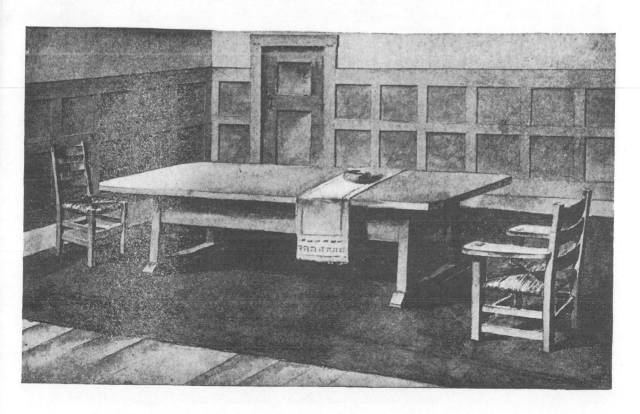

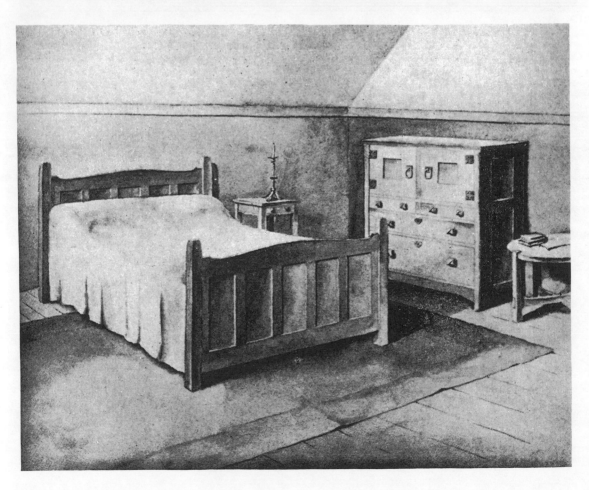

INFLUENCES AND EVOLUTION OF GUSTAV STICKLEY'S STYLE

Gustav Stickley has recently been elevated to the pinnacle of desirability among collectors of American Arts and Crafts furnishings. Much is being written in the way of aesthetic appraisal of the furniture and accessories produced by Stickley's factory from 1901 until 1915 but little modern writing describes his philosophical position at the turn of the century. His own words, reprinted in the following text, are the most objective evidence supporting claims to Gustav Stickley's pre-eminence as a cabinet-maker and proselytizer in his era.

In 1900 I stopped using the standard patterns and finishes, and began to make all kinds of furniture after my own designs, independently of what other people were doing, or of any necessity to fit my designs, woods and finishes to the product of any other factory. For about a year I experimented with more or less fantastic forms. My frequent journeys to Europe and close study of the growth of what is called L'Art Nouveau in France, Germany and Austria interested me much in the decorative use of plant-forms, and I followed the suggestion so far as to try the effect of my own conception of a very simple and primitive conventionalization of some of the familiar plant-forms in the designing of furniture. After experimenting with a number of pieces, such as small tables giving in their form a conventionalized suggestion of such plants as the mallow, the sunflower and the pansy, I abandoned the idea, convinced that such designs failed to satisfy because they were based on a purely decorative form that should never be used for anything whose sole reason for being is in its usefulness. Conventionalized plant-forms are beautiful and fitting when used solely for decoration, but any one who starts to make a piece of furniture with a decorative form in mind, starts at the wrong end. The sole consideration at the basis of the design must be the thing itself and not its ornamentation. It must be a chair, a table, a bookcase or a bed that fills its mission of usefulness as well as it possibly can; it must be well-proportioned and honestly constructed, as beautifully finished as is possible for the wood of which it is made, and as stable, commodious or comfortable as would be required in a perfect thing of its kind. If all these requirements are honestly fulfilled, there is little need of ornament, unless some touch of decoration is suggested by the construction of the piece itself. Any applied or dragged-in ornamentation soon grows tiresome in the case of furniture as in architecture, and the effect is still weaker when the piece itself is founded upon an ornamental form in the attempt to create a new model that shall be decorative.

So my experiments with plant-forms as applied to furniture were of short duration. The Arts and Crafts movement in England was more nearly in harmony with what I had in mind, but even that did not involve a return to the sturdy and primitive forms that were meant for usefulness alone, and I began to work along the lines of a direct application of the fundamental principals of structure to the designing and workmanship of my furniture. I took up the idea of plain forms as essentially structural and reasonable, and the Craftsman furniture of to-day is the result of the working out of that idea.

It has been, like everything else, a matter of growth. I tried flat forms first, but soon abandoned them in favor of the square, which I regard as a gain both in beauty and durability. Also, at first, I used an occasional touch of ornamentation, but gradually left off all decoration as the beauty of pure form developed and any kind of ornament became more and more to seem unnecessary and intrusive. The only decoration that seems in keeping with simple structural forms lies in the emphasizing of certain features of the construction, such as the mortise, tenon, key and dovetail. If these are added purely for the sake of decoration, they are as out of place as any other applied ornament; but where they really do the work for which they exist they are legit-

JOINERS   Craftsman Workshops, Eastwood, N. Y.

RUSH SEAT WORKERS   Craftsman Workshops, Eastwood, N. Y.

imately ornamental and add much to the strength of the piece as well as to its interest and beauty.

I am often asked whether I intend to continue making my plain furniture, or whether it is not likely to "go out of fashion" as other styles have done. It is not likely to go out of fashion, because it is not founded on fashion. When the honesty of plain, structural forms is once grasped by the mind there is little likelihood of change, for the reason that, once thoroughly understood, it is impossible to depart very far from it. Even the same forms, when made ornate, fail to appeal, and the only possible change lies in the further refining of the plain forms so that they come nearer to perfection. The Craftsman furniture is designed solely for use and comfort and durability, and the beauty that is peculiarly its own arises from the directness with which it meets these requirements as well as from the structural integrity of the design itself. Clumsiness and crudity are not and never have been a part of my idea. While a massive simplicity is the leading characteristic of the style, each piece is finely proportioned and as carefully finished as the work of the old Colonial cabinet-makers, and is as well-fitted to endure. It is my belief that simple, honest structural forms will prevail with but little modification for just so long as a practical, straightforward people asserts its own individuality sufficiently to demand that its home surroundings shall be practical, straightforward things.

Changes of fashion result from commercialism pure and simple, and the only things that remain unaffected are the things that are sufficiently vital and straightforward to be beyond the reach of commercialism. If what we make in the Craftsman Workshops has any value at all, that value will increase with every year of its existence, for it is founded upon our close adherence to principles that do not change.

DINING ROOM   Craftsman Building

LECTURE HALL   Craftsman Building

EXAMPLES OF EARLIEST CRAFTSMAN FURNITURE FROM "THE CRAFTSMAN"

The Craftsman, October 1901

The Craftsman, October 1901

The Craftsman, October 1901

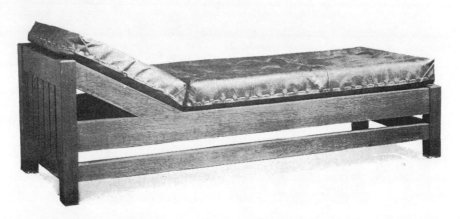

The Craftsman, October 1901

The Craftsman, November 1901

Small writing desk in green oak ; desk chair in same wood, with rush seat.

The Craftsman, November 1901

Work Cabinet in dark fumed oak ; hand-wrought copper hinges ; work basket in green rush ; cedar thread tray inside of drawer.

Sewing chair in dark fumed oak, with rush seat.

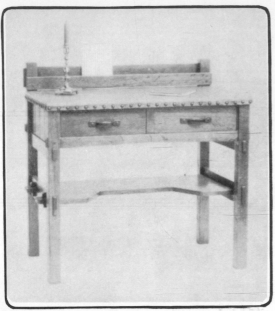

The Craftsman, November 1901

*Writing-table in gray oak ; top in sage green leather ;
wrought iron pulls.*

The Craftsman, November 1901

Book-cabinet in oak.

The Craftsman, November 1901

" The Thornden" rocker in fumed oak with rush seat.

The Craftsman, November 1901

*" The Eastwood " : large chair in fumed oak ; seat in United Crafts soft leather ;
Rest in same wood and leather.*

The Craftsman, November 1901

Smokers' cabinet and chair in dark oak ; chair cushion in United Crafts soft leather with laced edges.

The Craftsman, June 1902

Toilet Table by the United Crafts
The wood is oak, finished in '' driftwood '' effect : a blending of soft gray and old blue ; the drawer-pulls are in hand-wrought pewter, as are also the candlesticks which hold pale blue candles

The Craftsman, May 1902

Hall Clock by the United Crafts

The Craftsman, May 1902

Screen in fumed oak and United Crafts leather

The Craftsman, May 1902

Sideboard in fumed oak with wrought iron hinges, by the United Crafts Russian copper vessels in overhead cupboard

The Craftsman, June 1902

Bookcase, stool and rocker from the workshops of the United Crafts
The stool has a covering of sheepskin in a greenish shade ; the rocker seat is of uncolored raffia.   On the bookcase are
Russian copper vessels together with a candlestick of iron finished armor-bright with bands and rivets of hammered copper

The Craftsman, June 1902

Divan by the United Crafts
In fumed oak with cushion and pillows of sheepskin laced by hand with leather thongs

The Craftsman, June 1902

Bed in Austrian oak by the United Crafts
The blue and white homespun coverlet is a relic of Colonial days and is in pleasing contrast to the deep brown of the wood

The Craftsman, August 1902

The settle in the living-room.

The Craftsman, July 1902

Oaken Chest of Drawers, by the United Crafts

The Craftsman, July 1902

From the dining room of Mr. Gustave Stickley; nut-brown fumed oak, with copper hinges.

The Craftsman, July 1902

The Craftsman, July 1902

Buffet in brown fumed oak, by the United Crafts

The Craftsman, September 1902

Serving Table and Wine Cooler by the United Crafts.   Made in brown fumed oak with wrought copper trimmings.

Book case, in Green Oak, strap hinges in hammered copper
Chairs in same wood

The Craftsman, November 1902

Screen in chiselled leather.   Chairs in green oak

The Craftsman, November 1902

The Craftsman, July 1902
Dining Chairs in fumed oak, with seats woven in colored raffia, by the United Crafts

The Craftsman, July 1902
Arm Chair and Rocker in fumed oak, with seats woven in colored raffia, by the United Crafts

The Craftsman, August 1903

The Craftsman, August 1903

The Craftsman, May 1903

Hall Settle and Table, by Gustav Stickley

Arts and Crafts Exhibition
The Craftsman Building
Syracuse, N. Y.

SOCIAL IMPLICATIONS OF CRAFTSMAN FURNITURE

Stickley's concepts as he defined them are most obvious in his earliest experiments with furniture design. While reading this explanation or justification taken from a pamphlet called "Chips from the Workshop of Gustave Stickley" (1901), one should remember that Stickley was not addressing a receptive audience. The more profound aspects of an Arts and Crafts lifestyle were not wholeheartedly embraced by the majority of the American population. The newly rich did not respond to pleas for the subtle beauty of simplicity and the poor, in general, mirrored the showy excesses of the rich. Even if the average man was willing to "substitute the luxury of taste for the luxury of costliness" as Stickley admonished, he could not have afforded Craftsman furniture.

"Art, speaking broadly, may be defined as a creative operation of the intelligence; the making of something either with a view to utility or pleasure." This definition is given in one of the many elementary treatises of the day, which are designed to popularize knowledge. Accepting the definition and advancing a step farther, we may claim that artistic creations often attain a double end. They are useful and, at the same time, they afford keen sensuous pleasure. They minister to our physical needs and they deal with questions of harmony of line and color.

First of all, it should be recognized that, as has been well said by a great modern artist-artisan, luxury is the foe of art. This is the first and most stable principle among those which should be taught to the coming generation. And the second, in the form of a commandment from the same source of wisdom, is like unto it: "Have nothing in your houses that you do not know to be useful, or believe to be ornamental." In common with all other governing principles, these just named are to be accepted in spirit, rather than in letter.

In order, then, to bring on an age of artistic activity, of widely-diffused artistic knowledge, which shall be similar in character to the Middle Ages, the maker and user must understand and value each other. The maker must bend his energies to produce objects uniting in themselves the qualities of utility, of adaptability to place, of comfort, and of artistic effect. The user must choose with discretion the objects which shall create his home; carefully providing that they express his station in life and his own individuality; furthermore, that they respond to his every-day needs.

A question which rises just here, regards the number and use of the fittings necessary to the daily life of the middle class individual with whom we are so much concerned. First of all, we will consider the necessities of his living-room. They have been enumerated by the poet-artisan whom we have several times before quoted, and whose ennobling influence in household furnishings and decorations is acknowledged in both hemispheres. His list is a short one, for he inveighs against the crowding of the space necessary to convenience, health and beauty. First and most important is the bookcase; next, a table, firm and steady, adapted to writing, or working purposes; then, several chairs which shall be easily movable; and a comfortable couch, bench, seat, or settle, as it may be variously called; lastly, a desk, or cupboard provided with drawers; and a plant, or flower stand, especially if the room be located in a townhouse. In concluding, the authority makes a comment which should be considered by those who wish to live without friction and earnestly pursue their profession or calling. The comment is this: that we can add very little to these necessities without troubling ourselves and hindering our work, our thought, and our rest. It may also be added that as richness does not entail luxury—that foe of art and fore-runner of degeneracy—so simplicity does not necessitate cheapness, and that these objects should include none that have degraded a man to make, or to sell.

The Craftsman, November 1902
Book-cabinet in green oak; strap hinges and fittings in hammered copper

The Craftsman, April 1902

Living Room by The United Crafts

The Craftsman, June 1902

"The Craftsman House": Hall   *The Craftsman*, May 1903

"The Craftsman House": Library   *The Craftsman*, May 1903

Suggestions for Dining Room by the United Crafts

The Craftsman, May 1903

"The Craftsman House": Dining Room

The Craftsman, May 1902

The Craftsman, July 1902

A wall in the South chamber.

The Craftsman, May 1903

A LIBRARY IN AN ORDINARY HOUSE FITTED COMPLETELY WITH CRAFTSMAN FURNISHINGS.

The Craftsman, April 1902
Hall by The United Crafts

The Craftsman, October 1911
SHOWING THE CHARM OF A SQUARE HALLWAY FITTED ENTIRELY WITH CRAFTSMAN FURNISHINGS.

The Craftsman, October 1911
SECOND VIEW OF LIVING ROOM FITTED WITH CRAFTSMAN FURNISHINGS.

The Craftsman, October 1911
AN ORDINARY SQUARE LIVING ROOM FITTED WITH CRAFTSMAN FURNISHINGS: THE COM-
BINATION OF CRAFTSMAN WOOD AND WILLOW FURNITURE IS ESPECIALLY INTERESTING.

ACKNOWLEDGEMENT OF THE INFLUENCE OF WILLIAM MORRIS FROM "THE CRAFTSMAN"

The ideas promulgated by Gustav Stickley cannot be considered *avant garde.* In the foreword to the first issue of *The Craftsman* which appeared in October 1901, Stickley acknowledges his debt to the precepts of William Morris whose experiments in socialism began decades earlier.

With the initial number of "The Craftsman," The United Crafts of Eastwood, N.Y., enter upon a work for which they hope to gain the sympathy and the co-operation of a wide public. The new association is a guild of cabinet makers, metal and leather workers, which has been recently formed for the production of household furnishings. The Guild has had but one parallel in modern times, and this is found in the firm organized in London, in 1860, by the great decorator and socialist, William Morris, together with his not less distinguished friends, Burne-Jones, Rossetti and Ford Madox Brown, all of Pre-Raphaelite fame.

The United Crafts endeavor to promote and to extend the principles established by Morris, in both the artistic and the socialistic sense. In the interests of art, they seek to substitute the luxury of taste for the luxury of costliness; to teach that beauty does not imply elaboration or ornament; to employ only those forms and materials which make for simplicity, individuality and dignity of effect.

Another object which The United Crafts regard as desirable and possible of attainment is the union in one person of the designer and the workman. This principle, which was personally put in practice by Morris, extended throughout his workshops; the Master executing with his own hands what his brain had conceived, and the apprentice following the example set before him as far as his powers permitted. The divorce between theory and practice was everywhere strenuously opposed, with the direct aim of creating and perfecting the art-artisan. In accepting the Morris principle, the United Crafts recognize all that it implies: First: the raising of the general intelligence of the workman, by the increase of his leisure and the multiplication of his means of culture and pleasure. Second: a knowledge of drawing as a basis of all the manual arts and as one of the essentials of a primary education which shall be worthy of the name.

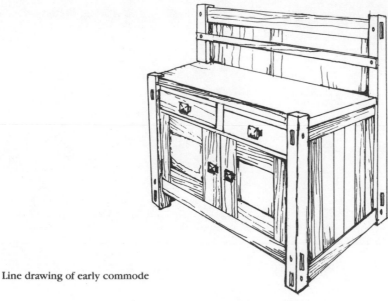

Line drawing of early commode

INLAID FURNITURE PRODUCED DURING THE TENURE OF HARVEY ELLIS

The delicate inlaid designs instigated by Harvey Ellis were a major departure from staunch Craftsman philosophy. Stickley gamely attempted to integrate them through an esoteric association with ancient Greek art. He claimed the feather-like motifs relieved what would otherwise be too large an area of a plain, flat surface. However, he later produced many of these designs without the embellishment of inlay.

This ornament, like that of the Greeks, appears to proceed from within outward. It bears no trace of having been applied. It consists of fine markings, discs, and other figures of pewter and copper, which, like the stems of plants and obscured, simplified floral forms, seem to pierce the surface of the wood from beneath. In the ornament of the cabinet work, the silvery lines with their expanded terminals of bright bronze or colored woods, contrast well with the gray-brown of the oak, which in every example shown provides the building material.

The Craftsman, January 1904

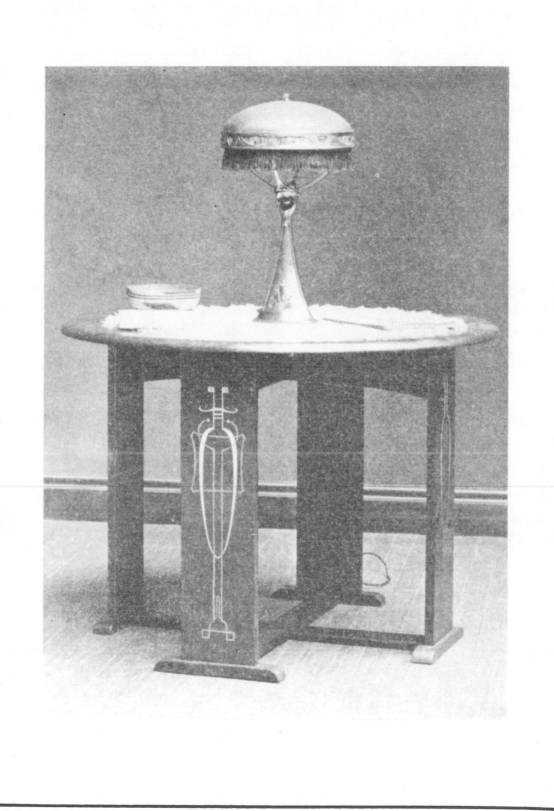

The Craftsman, January 1904

The Craftsman, January 1904

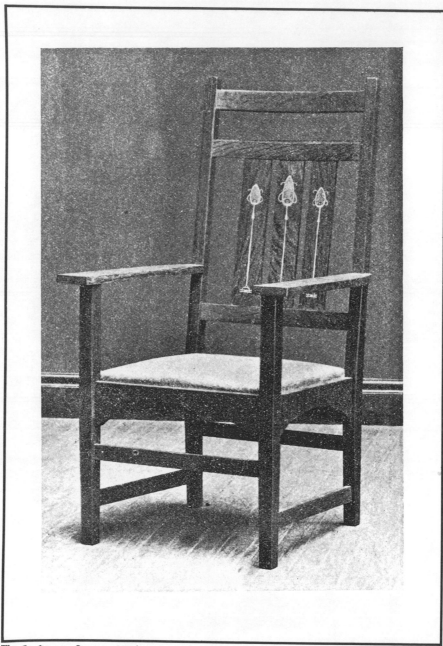

The Craftsman, January 1904

The Craftsman, January 1904

The Craftsman, January 1904

A CRAFTSMAN PIANO IN GRAY FUMED OAK

Craftsman Workshops

The Craftsman, October 1903

ORIGIN OF THE STICKLEY SIGNATURE

The United Crafts was a factory from its inception at Eastwood, New York. The stated similarity to medieval guilds was a necessary bit of propaganda and despite pictures of Gustav wielding a hammer in the blacksmith shop, one craftsman was not responsible for the entire production of an individual piece. "The Master of the Crafts" did not personally select the oak boards used in each piece of furniture nor did he actually sign and date each work. The famous red compass and motto appeared, most often, as an ephemeral decal.

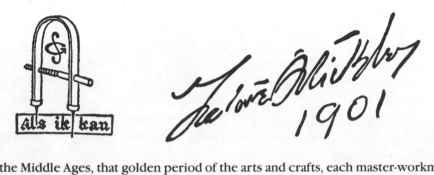

In the Middle Ages, that golden period of the arts and crafts, each master-workman adopted some device or legend which, displayed upon every object of his creation, came finally to represent his individuality as completely as did his face, or his voice; making him known beyond the burgher circle in which he passed his life, and, after his death, becoming a magic formula, by which to conjure up his memory, even though the years had multiplied into centuries.

Among the legends so employed, the one assumed by Ian van Eyck, the early Flemish painter, has retained its force and point down to our own day. *Als ich kanne* (if I can) appears written across the canvases of this fourteenth century *chef d'ecole,* placed there, without doubt, as an inspiration toward excellence in that art wherein van Eyck became an epoch maker. Appearing in the background of his masterful portraits, it has something of defiance and humor, as if offering a covert challenge to less skillful limners.

The *Als ich kanne* of van Eyck, like the *Quand meme* of Sarah Bernhardt, reflects that sentiment of courage, boldness and persistency which apppeals to all truly virile natures. Thus when William Morris, in his early manhood, visited the Low Countries, and there grew fired with enthusiasm for the decorative arts, he found this legend and made it his own. He used it, in French translation, first in tapestries designed for his own dwelling, and finally it became identified with him; so that the *Si je puis* now recalls his memory as vividly as do the designs which speak to us from the hangings of our walls, the tiles of our floors, or the covers of the books which lie upon our tables.

The same legend in its modern Flemish form, *Als ik kan* has been adopted by the Master of the United Crafts. It here forms an interesting device with a joiner's compass, which is the most primitive and distinctive tool of the worker in wood. The legend is further accompanied by the signature of the Master of the Crafts, Gustave Stickley, which, together with the proper date, appears branded upon every object produced in the workshop of the Guild.

In this way, authenticity is assured, comparisons of progress are made possible, and every facility of information is afforded to the one who shall acquire the piece.

CABINET WORK
FROM
THE CRAFTSMAN
WORKSHOPS

SETTLE

Number 210

Made in Craftsman Fumed Oak. 36" high, 84" long, 34" deep. Seat cushion covered in Craftsman canvas or leather. The size of seat cushion is such that only one out of every one hundred hides is large enough to cover it. This is our largest settle, and the only piece we ship "knocked down." It is long enough to allow the body to recline at full length. The tenons projecting through the front and back posts are pinned, and form a pleasing decoration.

Pillows not included in price
Craftsman Canvas, . . $75.50
Craftsman Leather, . . 96.50

9

SETTLE

Number 207

Made in Craftsman Fumed Oak. 39″ high, 70″ long, 34″ deep. Seat cushion covered in Craftsman canvas or leather. This settle is roomy and exceedingly comfortable, adapted for use in large living rooms.

Pillows not included in price
Craftsman Canvas, . . $63.50
Craftsman Leather, . . 83.50

10

SETTLE

Number 208

Made in Craftsman Fumed Oak. 29″ high, 76″ long, 32″ deep. Seat cushion covered in Craftsman canvas or leather. The back and ends form a natural rest for arms and head, when supported by pillows. The tenons of the side rails projecting through back and front posts are a pleasing feature.

Pillows not included in price
Craftsman Canvas, , . $57.00
Craftsman Leather, . . 78.00

11

C O U C H

Number 216

Made in Craftsman Fumed Oak. 29″ high, 79″ long, 31″ deep. Seat cushion covered in Craftsman canvas or leather. Two fitted pillows add to comfort and restfulness. Seat cushion best adapted to leather covering, although canvas may be used.

Pillows not included in price

Craftsman Canvas, . . $46.50
Craftsman Leather, . . 58.00

12

H A L L   S E T T L E

Number 205

Made in Craftsman Fumed Oak. 30″ high, 56″ long, 22″ deep. Seat cushion covered in Craftsman canvas or leather. This settle is intended for use in entrance halls or small nooks.

Craftsman Canvas, . . $36.00
Craftsman Leather, . . 46.00

13

S E T T L E

Number 206

Made in Craftsman Fumed Oak. 40″ high, 60″ long, 28″ deep. Seat cushion covered in Craftsman canvas or leather. This has the highest back of any of our settles, is comfortable and well adapted for use in a medium-sized living-room or library.

Pillows not included in price

Craftsman Canvas,	. .	$52.50
Craftsman Leather,	. .	69.50

14

S E T T L E

Number 213

Made in Craftsman Fumed Oak, Silver Gray Maple or Mahogany. $30\frac{1}{2}$″ high, 78″ long, 30″ deep. This piece looks especiallly well cushioned in Craftsman canvas with appliqued pillows, as shown in plate. Craftsman leather may be used. The size affords ample room for reclining at full length.

Pillows not included in price

Craftsman Canvas

Oak	Maple	Mahogany
$51.00	$54.00	$58.75

Craftsman Leather

Oak	Maple	Mahogany
$71.00	$74.00	$78.75

15

S E T T L E

Number 214

Made in Craftsman Fumed Oak, Silver Gray Maple or Mahogany. $30\frac{1}{2}''$ high, $50''$ long, $27''$ deep. This piece looks especially well cushioned in Craftsman canvas with appliqued pillows as shown in plate. Craftsman leather may also be used.

Pillows not included in price

Craftsman Canvas

Oak	Maple	Mahogany
$40.50	$42.75	$46.00

Craftsman Leather

Oak	Maple	Mahogany
$49.00	$51.25	$54.50

16

A R M C H A I R

Number 328

Made in Craftsman Fumed Oak, Silver Gray Maple or Mahogany. This piece looks especially well cushioned in Craftsman canvas with appliqued back cushion, as shown in plate. Craftsman leather may also be used.

Built on lighter lines to correspond with No. 213 or No. 214 settles.

Height of back from floor, 28″
Height of seat   "   "   17″
Size of seat, 23″ wide, 25″ deep

Craftsman Canvas

Oak	Maple	Mahogany
$21.00	$22.00	$23.75

Craftsman Leather

Oak	Maple	Mahogany
$28.00	$29.00	$30.75

17

RECLINING CHAIR

Number 332

Made in Craftsman Fumed Oak; adjustable back. Seat and back cushions covered in Craftsman canvas or leather. Generous in its proportions and built essentially for comfort.

Height of back from floor, 40″
Height " seat " " 15″
Size of seat, 23″ wide, 27″ deep

Craftsman Canvas . . $26.50
Craftsman Leather . . 33.00

18

RECLINING CHAIR

Number 336

Made in Craftsman Fumed Oak or Mahogany. Adjustable back. Seat and back cushions covered in Craftsman canvas or leather. A good reading chair.

Height of back from floor, 39″
Height of seat " " 14″
Size of seat, 22″ wide, 23″ deep.

Craftsman Canvas
Oak   Mahogany
$26.00 $29.50

Craftsman Leather
Oak   Mahogany
$31.50 $35.00

19

RECLINING CHAIR

Number 334

Made in Craftsman Fumed Oak or Mahogany. Adjustable back. Seat and back cushions covered in Craftsman canvas or leather. Heavy saddlery leather suspended on rails from front to back, forms a practical arrangement for supporting seat cushion.

Height of back from floor, 37″
Height of seat from floor, 17″
Size of seat, 21″ wide, 23″ deep

Craftsman Canvas
Oak	Mahogany
$26.00	$29.75

Craftsman Leather
Oak	Mahogany
$31.50	$35.25

20

RECLINING CHAIR

Number 346

Made in Craftsman Fumed Oak or Mahogany. Adjustable back. Seat and back cushions covered in Craftsman canvas or leather.

Height of back from floor, 41″
Height of seat   "   "   16″
Size of seat, 21″ wide, 23″ deep.

Craftsman Canvas
Oak	Mahogany
$22.50	$26.00

Craftsman Leather
Oak	Mahogany
$26.00	$29.50

21

ARM ROCKER

Number 323

Made in Craftsman Fumed Oak or Mahogany. Seat and back cushions covered in Craftsman canvas or leather. Generous proportions for comfort.

Height of back from floor, 36″
Height of seat from floor, 16″
Size of seat, 22″ wide, 25″ deep

Craftsman Canvas

Oak	Mahogany
$22.00	$25.00

Craftsman Leather

Oak	Mahogany
$28.00	$31.00

22

ARM CHAIR

Number 324

Height of back from floor, 29″
Height " seat " " 16″

Companion piece to
No. 323 Rocker.

Craftsman Canvas

Oak	Mahogany
$22.00	$25.00

Craftsman Leather

Oak	Mahogany
$28.00	$31.00

23

R O C K E R

Number 319

Made in Craftsman Fumed Oak or Mahogany. Seat and back cushions covered in Craftsman canvas or leather. A man's rocker, deep and roomy.

Height of back from floor, 38″
Height " seat " " 15″
Size of seat, 21″ wide, 23″ deep

Craftsman Canvas

Oak	Mahogany
$19.00	$21.25

Craftsman Leather

Oak	Mahogany
$24.50	$26.75

24

C H A I R

Number 320

Height of back from floor, 42″
Height of seat " " 17″

Companion piece to No. 319 Rocker.

Craftsman Canvas

Oak	Mahogany
$19.00	$21.25

Craftsman Leather

Oak	Mahogany
$24.50	$26.75

25

A R M   R O C K E R

Number 315

Made in Craftsman Fumed Oak. Cushion covered in Craftsman leather or canvas.

The cushion and high back combine to make this rocker very comfortable.

Height of back from floor,   38″
Height of seat   "   "   15″
Size of seat, 20″ wide, 18″ deep.

Craftsman Canvas
Oak, ... $14.00
Craftsman Leather,
Oak, ... $17.00

26

C H A I R

Number 316

Height of back from floor,   40″
Height of seat   "   "   18″

Companion piece to No. 315 Rocker.

Craftsman Canvas
Oak, ... $14.00
Craftsman Leather
Oak, ... $17.00

27

A R M   R O C K E R

Number 317

Made in Craftsman Fumed Oak. Cushion covered in Craftsman canvas or leather. The high back forms a very comfortable head rest.

Height of back from floor,   38″
Height of seat   "   "   15″
Size of seat, 19″ wide, 19″ deep

Craftsman Canvas, . . $13.50
Craftsman Leather, . .   16.50

28

A R M   C H A I R

Number 318

Height of back from floor, 38″
Height " seat " " 18″

Companion piece to No. 317
Rocker.

Craftsman Canvas, . . $13.50
Craftsman Leather, . .   16.5ò

29

A R M   C H A I R

Number 330

Made in Craftsman Fumed Oak, Silver Gray Maple or Mahogany. This piece looks well cushioned in Craftsman canvas, with or without appliqued design on back cushion. Craftsman leather may be used. Built on lighter lines to correspond with No. 213 or No. 214 settles.

Height of back from floor,   39″
Height of seat   "   "   16″
Size of seat, 21″ wide, 23″ deep

Craftsman Canvas		
Oak	Maple	Mahogany
$23.00	$24.25	$26.00
Craftsman Leather		
Oak	Maple	Mahogany
$31.00	$32.25	$34.00

30

A R M   R O C K E R

Number 311

Craftsman Fumed Oak. Rush or Sheepskin seat. Height of back from floor, 35″; height of seat from floor, 15″; seat, 21″ wide, 18″ deep.
Price, ... $10.00

ARM ROCKER

Number 311½

Craftsman Fumed Oak or Mahogany. Craftsman leather seat. Same design and dimensions as No. 311.
Oak $11.50   Mahogany $14.25

ARM CHAIR

Number 312

Craftsman Fumed Oak. Rush or Sheepskin seat. Height of back from floor, 36″; height of seat from floor, 18″; seat, 21″ wide, 18″ deep.
Price, ... $10.00

ARM CHAIR

Number 312½

Craftsman Fumed Oak or Mahogany. Craftsman leather seat. Same design and dimensions as No. 312.
Oak $11.50   Mahogany $14.25

31

R O C K E R
Number 303

Made in Craftsman Fumed Oak or Mahogany. Cushion covered in Craftsman canvas or leather. Our lowest and most comfortable rocker for a mother's use.

Height of back from floor, 33″
Height of seat " " 14″
Size of seat, 16″ wide, 16″ deep

Craftsman Canvas
Oak   Mahogany
$9.00 $10.50

Craftsman Leather
Oak   Mahogany
$10.00 $11.50

C H A I R
Number 304

Well designed for hall or reception room.

Height of back from floor, 36″
Height of seat " " 17″

Craftsman Canvas
Oak   Mahogany
$9.00 $10.50

Craftsman Leather
Oak   Mahogany
$10.00 $11.50

32

A R M R O C K E R
Number 339

Made in Craftsman Fumed Oak, Silver Gray Maple or Mahogany. Slip seat in Craftsman leather or rush.

Height of back from floor, 36″
Height of seat " " 14″

Size of seat, 18″ wide, 16″ deep
Light and comfortable.

Oak   Maple   Mahogany
$10.75 $11.75 $13.50

A R M C H A I R
Number 340

Matches No. 339 Rocker

Height of back from floor, 18″
Height of seat " " 41″
Size of seat, 18″ wide, 16″ deep

Oak   Maple   Mahogany
$10.75 $11.75 $13.50

33

SMALL ROCKER

Number 337

Made in Craftsman Fumed Oak, Silver Gray Maple or Mahogany. Slip seat in Craftsman leather or rush.

Height of back from floor, 35"
Height of seat " " 13"
Size of seat, 15" wide, 14" deep

Designed to be used with our lighter pieces.

Oak	Maple	Mahogany
$7.75	$8.50	$9.75

SMALL CHAIR

Number 338

Matches No. 337 Rocker

Height of back from floor, 40"
Height of seat " " 18"
Size of seat, 15" wide, 14" deep

Oak	Maple	Mahogany
$7.75	$8.50	$9.75

34

ARM ROCKER

Number 309

Craftsman Fumed Oak, Silver Gray Maple or Mahogany. Rush or Sheepskin seat. Height of back from floor, 32"; height of seat from floor, 15". Size of seat, 20" wide, 19" deep.

Oak $8.75 Maple $9.50 Mahog. $11.00

ARM ROCKER
Number 309½

Craftsman Fumed Oak, Silver Gray Maple or Mahogany, Craftsman leather Design and dimensions like No. 309.

Oak, $10.25 Maple, $11.25 Mahog. $12.75

ARM CHAIR
Number 310

Craftsman Fumed Oak, Silver Gray Maple or Mahogany. Rush, or Sheepskin seat. Height of back from floor, 36"; height of seat from floor, 18". Size of seat, 20" wide, 19" deep.

Oak, $8.75 Maple, $9.50 Mahog. $11.00

ARM CHAIR
Number 310½

Craftsman Fumed Oak, Silver Gray Maple or Mahogany, Craftsman leather. Design and dimensions like No. 310.

Oak $10.25 Maple $11.25 Mahog. $12.75

35

ROCKER
Number 305½

Craftsman Fumed Oak or Mahogany. Craftsman leather. Height of back from floor, 31″; height of seat from floor, 14″; seat, 16″ x 16″.

Oak $6.00   Mahogany $7.50

CHAIR
Number 306½

Matches No. 305½ Rocker. Height of back from floor, 36″; height of seat from floor, 18″.

Oak $6.00   Mahogany $7.50

ROCKER
Number 305

Design and dimensions same as No. 305½. Rush, or Sheepskin seat.

Oak $5.00   Maple $5.50   Mahogany $6.25

CHAIR
Number 306

Design and dimensions same as No. 306½. Rush or Sheepskin seat.

Oak $5.00   Maple $5.50   Mahogany $6.25

36

SEAT OR FOOT-REST
Number 300

Made in Craftsman Fumed Oak or Mahogany, covered in Craftsman leather.

Height of seat from floor, 15″
Size of seat, 20″ wide, 16″ deep

Oak   Mahogany
$7.50 $9.25

SEAT OR FOOT-REST
Number 301

Made in Craftsman Fumed Oak, Silver Gray Maple or Mahogany. Hand-made rush, or sheepskin seat.

Height of seat from floor, 17½″
Size of seat, 20″ wide, 16″ deep

A convenient seat for ladies' toilet table.

Oak   Maple   Mahogany
$6.00 $6.50 $7.50

37

CHILD'S ARM ROCKER

Number 343

Made in Craftman Fumed Oak or Silver Gray Maple. Seat covered in Craftsman canvas.

Height of back from floor, 24″
Height of seat " " 11″
Size of seat, 15″ wide, 13″ deep

Strong enough to stand hard usage.

Oak	Maple
$3.75	$4.00

CHILD'S ARM CHAIR

Number 344

Height of back from floor, 25″
Height of seat " " 11″

Companion piece to No, 343.

Oak	Maple
$3.75	$4.00

38

CHILD'S SMALL ROCKER

Number 341

Made in Craftsman Fumed Oak or Silver Gray Maple. Seat covered in Craftsman canvas.

Height of back from floor, 23″
Height of seat " " 11″
Size of seat, 13″ wide, 13″ deep

So light that the child can easily carry it.

Oak	Maple
$2.75	$3.00

CHILD'S SMALL CHAIR

Number 342

Height of back from floor, 23″
Height of seat " " 11″

Companion piece to No. 341.

Oak	Maple
$2.75	$3.00

39

CHILD'S SETTLE

Number 215

Made in Craftsman Fumed Oak or Silver Gray Maple, with wood seat. 38" long, 15" deep.

Height of back from floor, 31"
Height of seat " " 13"

Designed for use with No. 639 table.

A practical piece, simple in design.

Oak	Maple
$6.50	$7.25

CHILD'S TABLE

Number 639

Made in Craftsman Fumed Oak or Silver Gray Maple, 22" high, top 24" x 36". An attractive luncheon and play table for nursery or kindergarten.

Oak	Maple
$6.50	$7.25

40

TABOURET

Number 601

Made in Craftsman Fumed Oak. Wood Top. 16" high, 14" diameter.

Price, ... $3.75

TABOURET

Number 602

Made in Craftsman Fumed Oak. Wood Top. 18" high, 16" diameter. A useful piece of furniture in any room.

Price, ... $4.25

TABOURET

Number 603

Made in Craftsman Fumed Oak. Wood Top. 20" high, 18" diameter. Of sufficient size to hold large Jardiniere.

Price, ... $5.00

41

TEA TABLE

Number 604

Made in Craftsman Fumed Oak. Wood, or Craftsman leather top.

26″ high, 20″ diameter.

Of convenient size for drink or smoker's stand.

Wood Top, ... $ 6.75
Hard Leather Top, . . 11.50

42

ROUND TABLE

Number 607

Made in Craftsman Fumed Oak. Wood, or Craftsman leather top.

29″ high, 24″ diameter.

Wood Top, ... $10.50
Leather Top, ... 15.00

ROUND TABLE

Number 609

Made in Craftsman Fumed Oak. Wood, or Craftsman leather top. Like No. 607 in design.

A good centre-table.
29″ high, 36″ diameter.

Wood Top, ... $19.50
Leather Top, ... 28.50

43

SQUARE TABLE

Number 611

Made in Craftsman Fumed Oak. Wood, or Craftsman leather top.

Desirable in bedrooms.
29″ high; top 24″ x 24″.

Wood Top, ... $10.50
Leather Top, ... 15.00

SQUARE TABLE

Number 612

Made in Craftsman Fumed Oak. Wood, or Craftsman leather top.

Like No. 611 in design.
29″ high; top 30″ x 30″

Wood Top, ... $15.00
Leather Top, ... 21.50

44

LIBRARY TABLE

Number 613

Made in Craftsman Fumed Oak. Wood, or Craftsman leather top. Hand-wrought pulls in iron or copper.

30″ high; top, 24 x 36″.

Wood Top, ... $24.00
Leather Top, ... 33.00

45

LIBRARY TABLE

Number 614

Made in Craftsman Fumed Oak.
Wood, or Craftsman leather top.
Hand-wrought pulls in iron or
copper.

30″ high, 42″ long, 30″ wide.

Wood Top, ...	$30.00
Leather Top, ...	42.50

LIBRARY TABLE

Number 615

Made in Craftsman Fumed Oak.
Wood or Craftsman leather top.
Hand-wrought pulls in iron or
copper.

Like No. 614 in design.

30″ high, 48″ long, 30″ wide.

Wood Top, ...	$38.00
Leather Top, ...	52.00

46

LIBRARY TABLE

Number 616

Made in Craftsman Fumed
Oak. Wood, or Craftsman
leather top. Hand-wrought
pulls in iron or copper.

Well designed for library or
living room.

30″ high, 54″ long, 32″ wide

Wood Top, ...	$42.00
Leather Top, ...	58.50

47

LIBRARY TABLE

Number 619

Made in Craftsman Fumed Oak. Wood, or Craftsman leather top. Hand-wrought pulls in iron or copper. Handsome table for large library or living room.

30″ high, 66″ long, 36″ wide

Wood Top, ...	$52.00
Leather Top, . . .	76.00

48

LIBRARY TABLE

Number 649

Made in Craftsman Fumed Oak, Silver Gray Maple or Mahogany. Wood, or Craftsman leather top. Hand-wrought pulls in iron, copper or old brass. Desirable for use with lighter pieces.

29″ high, 36″ long, 24″ wide

Wood Top		
Oak	Maple	Mahogany
$22.00	$24.25	$27.50

Leather Top	
Oak, ...	$31.00

49

ROUND TABLE

Number 648

Made in Craftsman Fumed Oak. Wood, or Craftsman leather top. Desirable for nursery, as it may be used for centre and lunch-table.

30″ high, 36″ diameter

Wood Top, ... $14.50
Leather Top, ... $21.00

50

ROUND TABLE

Number 626

Made in Craftsman Fumed Oak. Wood, or Craftsman leather top. A good chafing-dish table.

30″ high, 40″ diameter

Wood Top, ... $18.50
Leather Top, ... 29.50

ROUND TABLE

Number 627

Made in Craftsman Fumed Oak. Wood, or Craftsman leather top. Design like No. 626 table. It is our most suitable table with solid top for dining room use.

30″ high, 48″ diameter
Wood Top, ... $26.00
Leather Top, ... 43.50

51

LUNCH TABLE

Number 647

Made in Craftsman Fumed Oak. Wood, or Craftsman leather top. A practical and inexpensive table for use in any room, club or cafe.

30″ high, 28″ wide, 40″ long

Wood Top, ... $15.00
Leather Top, ... 27.00

52

ROUND TABLE
Number 644
Made in Craftsman Fumed Oak, Silver Gray Maple or Mahogany. The posts extending on outside through top are attractive ; they do not interfere with cover if one is used.
29″ high, 30″ diameter

Oak	Maple	Mahogany
$12.00	$13.25	$15.00

ROUND TABLE
Number 645
Made in Craftsman Fumed Oak, Silver Gray Maple or Mahogany. Design same as No. 644 table.
29″ high, 36″ diameter

Oak	Maple	Mahogany
$16.00	$17.50	$20.00

ROUND TABLE
Number 646
Made in Craftsman Fumed Oak, Silver Gray Maple or Mahogany. A good centre or small library table. Design same as No. 644.
29″ high, 40″ diameter

Oak	Maple	Mahogany
$20.00	$22.00	$25.00

53

LIBRARY TABLE

Number 650

Made in Craftsman Fumed Oak, Silver Gray Maple or Mahogany. Wood, or Craftsman leather top. Hand-wrought pulls in iron, copper or old brass.

29″ high, 48″ long, 30″ wide

Wood Top		
Oak	Maple	Mahogany
$35.00	$38.50	$43.75
Leather Top		
Oak, ...		$49.00

54

LIBRARY TABLE

Number 651

Made in Craftsman Fumed Oak. Wood, or Craftsman leather top. ~~Hand-wrought pulls in iron or copper~~. Desirable for use in a medium-sized living-room.

30″ high, 30″ wide, 48″ long

Wood Top, ...	$22.00
Leather Top, ...	36.00

55

LIBRARY TABLE

Number 637

Made in Craftsman Fumed Oak. Wood, or Craftsman leather top. This table-base differs from that of most of our tables, being more decorative in design, but it is fully as structural.

20″ high, 48″ long, 30″ wide

Wood Top, ...	$22.00
Leather Top, ...	36.00

56

LIBRARY TABLE

Number 635

Made in Craftsman Fumed Oak. Wood, or Craftsman leather top. The tenons are keyed, adding a pleasing decorative feature. The overhanging top affords ample knee-room.

29″ high, 40″ diameter

Wood Top, ...	$25.00
Leather Top, ...	36.00

LIBRARY TABLE

Number 636

Made in Craftsman Fumed Oak. Wood, or Craftsman leather top. Design same as No. 635 table.

29″ high, 48″ diameter

Wood Top, ...	$30.00
Leather Top, ...	46.00

57

LIBRARY TABLE

Number 625

Made in Craftsman Fumed Oak. Wood, or Craftsman leather top. The three stretchers are an unusual and attractive feature. The tenons projecting through the legs are pinned, forming a pleasing decoration.

29" high, 48" hexagonal

Wood Top, ... $41.50
Leather Top, ... 58.50

58

SEWING TABLE

Number 630

Made in Craftsman Fumed Oak. Till in top drawer. Handwrought pulls in iron or copper. A quaint and useful piece of furniture.

26" high, 16" x 16" closed

Price, ... $20.50

SMALL ROCKER

Number 337

Made in Craftsman Fumed Oak, Silver Gray Maple or Mahogany. Slip seat in Craftsman leather or rush. A companion piece to No. 338 chair.

Height of back from floor, 35"
Height of seat "   "   13"
Size of seat, 15" wide, 14" deep

Oak	Maple	Mahogany
$7.75	$8.50	$9.75

59

CARD TABLE

Number 643

CLOSED

Made in Craftsman Fumed Oak. Automatic Reversible Top, reverse side covered in Craftsman leather. When not in use for cards, it may be utilized as a centre-table. The stretchers, tenons and pins are good features.

$29\frac{1}{2}''$ high, 42'' diameter

Price, ... $51.00

60

CARD TABLE

Number 643

OPEN

Made in Craftsman Fumed Oak. Automatic Reversible Top, card side covered in Craftsman leather; and which is secured by invisible brass hinges and push-spring lock. It covers compartments for the storing of cards; chips, etc.

$29\frac{1}{2}''$ high, 42'' diameter

Price, ... $51.00

61

DROP-LEAF TABLE

Number 638

Made in Craftsman Fumed Oak. In rooms where space has to be considered this table is invaluable, as it can be closed, taking up small space, and opened when necessary, for writing, etc. A desirable table for students.

30″ high; top closed, 40″ x 14″; top open, 40″ x 42″.

Price, ... $18.00

62

WRITING TABLE

Number 720

Made in Craftsman Fumed Oak, Silver Gray Maple or Mahogany. Two good-sized drawers with hand-wrought pulls in iron, copper or old brass. Convenient arrangement of small drawers, pigeon - holes and pencil racks.

38″ high, 38″ wide, 21″ deep

Oak	Maple	Mahogany
$23.50	$25.75	$29.25

63

LADIES' DESK

Number 724

CLOSED

Made in Craftsman Fumed Oak, Silver Gray Maple or Mahogany. Trimmed in hand-wrought iron, copper or old brass; panelled lid. Interior finished any desired color, and conveniently arranged with small drawer and pigeon-holes. Especially desirable for use with lighter pieces.

46″ high, 32″ wide, 12″ deep

Oak	Maple	Mahogany
$26.00	$38.50	$32.50

64

LADIES' DESK

Number 724

OPEN

Made in Craftsman Fumed Oak, Silver Gray Maple or Mahogany, trimmed in hand-wrought iron, copper or old brass; panelled lid. Interior finished any desired color. Conveniently arranged with small drawer, and pigeon holes. Especially desirable for use with lighter pieces.

46″ high, 32″ wide, 12″ deep

Oak	Maple	Mahogany
$26.00	$28.50	$32.50

65

L A D I E S '   D E S K

Number 706

CLOSED

Made in Craftsman Fumed Oak, Silver Gray Maple or Mahogany, trimmed in hand-wrought iron, copper or old brass. Panelled lid; good lock. Interior finished any desired color. Conveniently fitted with pigeon-holes, small drawers, pencil rack and ink-wells.

44″ high, 30″ wide, 11″ deep.

Oak	Maple	Mahogany
$30.00	$33.00	$37.50

66

L A D I E S '   D E S K

Number 706

OPEN

Made in Craftsman Fumed Oak, Silver Gray Maple or Mahogany, trimmed in hand-wrought iron, copper or old brass. Panelled lid; good lock. Interior finished any desired color. Conveniently fitted with pigeon-holes, small drawers, pencil rack and ink-wells.

44″ high, 30″ wide, 11″ deep.

Oak	Maple	Mahogany
$30.00	$33.00	$37.50

67

SMALL DESK

Number 705

CLOSED

Made in Craftsman Fumed Oak, trimmed in hand-wrought iron or copper. Panelled lid; good lock. Interior finished any desired color, and conveniently fitted with pigeon-holes, small drawer, etc. A compact desk with every inch of space utilized.

52″ high, 26″ wide, 14″ deep.

Price, ... $28.00

68

SMALL DESK

Number 705

OPEN

Made in Craftsman Fumed Oak, trimmed in hand-wrought iron or copper. Panelled lid; good lock. Interior finished any desired color, and conveniently fitted with pigeon-holes, small drawer, etc. A compact desk with every inch of space utilized.

52″ high, 26″ wide, 14″ deep.

Price, ... $28.00

69

WRITING DESK

Number 708

Made in Craftsman Fumed Oak. Wood, or Craftsman leather top. Hand-wrought pulls in iron or copper. Two racks. Ample writing surface, with broad shelf beneath that does not interfere with knee-room.

30″ high, 40″ wide, 22″ deep.

Wood Top, ... $23.50
Leather Top, ... 35.00

70

TABLE DESK

Number 709

Made in Craftsman Fumed Oak or Mahogany. Wood, or Craftsman leather top. Panelled sides and back. Hand-wrought pulls in iron, copper or old brass. Yale lock on centre drawer; writing surface of ample proportions. An addition to any library. Wood Top.

29″ high, 42″ long, 24″ wide.
Wood Top

Oak	Mahogany
$38.00	$47.50

Leather Top
Oak, ... $48.00

TABLE DESK

Number 710

Made only in Craftsman Fumed Oak.
Design like No. 709.
30″ high, 44″ long, 28″ wide.
Oak
Wood Top, ... $45.00
Leather Top, ... 57.00

71

LIBRARY TABLE DESK
Number 711

Made in Craftsman Fumed Oak or Mahogany. Wood or Craftsman leather top. Panelled sides and back. Yale lock on centre-drawer. Hand-wrought pulls in iron, copper or old brass. Ample drawer space.

30" high, 60" long, 32" deep.

Wood Top

Oak	Mahogany
$70.00	$87.50

Leather Top

Oak, . . . , . . . $93.00

LIBRARY DESK
Number 726

Made in Craftsman Fumed Oak or Mahogany, Wood, or Craftsman leather top.

30" high, 48" long, 28" deep.

A lighter model of No. 711, but of the same design.

Wood Top

Oak	Mahogany
$60.00	$75.00

Leather Top

Oak, . . , ... $80.00

WRITING DESK

Number 712

Made in Craftsman Fumed Oak or Mahogany. Panelled sides and back; five large drawers, ten small ones. Yale lock on center drawer; two arm slides; handsome hand-wrought pulls in iron, copper or old brass. Writing surface of ample proportions. A beautiful piece of furniture, which will lend dignity to any Library or Office.

36" high, 32" wide, 60" long

Oak	Mahogany
$90.00	$112.50

73

ROLL TOP DESK

Number 713

CLOSED

Made in Craftsman Fumed Oak. Panelled back and sides. Yale lock on Roll, centre-drawer and four small interior drawers; two arm slides; hand-wrought pulls in iron or copper. Ample writing surface. Interior conveniently arranged with small drawers and pigeon-holes.

46″ high, 60″ long, 32″ deep

Price, ... $115.00

75

ROLL TOP DESK

Number 713

OPEN

Made in Craftsman Fumed Oak. Panelled back and sides. Yale lock on Roll, centre-drawer and four small interior drawers; two arm slides; hand-wrought pulls in iron or copper. Ample writing surface. Interior conveniently arranged with small drawers and pigeon-holes.

46″ high, 60″ long, 32″ deep

Price, ... $115.00

74

BOOK SHELF AND CABINET

Number 722

Made in Craftsman Fumed Oak, trimmed in hand-wrought iron or copper. Adjustable shelves for books in frequent use. Good lock on Cabinet door. Cabinet also fitted with adjustable shelves.

45″ high, 38″ wide, 12″ deep.

Price, ... $24.00

76

ONE DOOR BOOK CASE

Number 715

Made in Craftsman Fumed Oak; clear glass squares set in sash. Combination hand-wrought pull and lock in iron or copper.

56″ high. 13″ deep, 36″ wide

Price, ... $26.00

77

TWO DOOR BOOK-CASES

Numbers 716 to 719

Made in Craftsman Fumed Oak; center partitions. Clear glass squares set in sash. All 56″ in height, 13″ in depth. Combination hand-wrought pull and locks, in iron or copper.

No. 716—42″ wide, . . $33.00

No. 717—48″ wide, . . 37.50

No. 718—54″ wide, . . 41.50

No. 719—60″ wide, . . 45.50

78

ONE DOOR BOOK CASE

Number 700

Made in Craftsman Fumed Oak, Silver Gray Maple or Mahogany. Door with leaded glass squares at top, and clear glass panels. Four adjustable shelves with capacity for 150 volumes.

58″ high,   36″ wide,   14″ deep

Oak	Maple	Mahogany
$28.00	$30.75	$33.00

79

TWO DOOR BOOK-CASES

Numbers 701 to 704

Made in Craftsman Fumed Oak, Silver Gray Maple or Mahogany. Leaded squares and clear glass panels. Center partitions and adjustable shelves. All 58″ inches in height, 14″ in depth.

No. 701—42″ wide

Oak	Maple	Mahogany
$35.00	$38.50	$48.00

No. 702—48″ wide

Oak	Maple	Mahogany
$39.50	$43.50	$54.00

No. 703—54″ wide

Oak	Maple	Mahogany
$43.50	$47.75	$59.50

No. 704—60″ wide

Oak	Maple	Mahogany
$47.50	$52.25	$65.00

80

OFFICE ARM CHAIR

Number 364

Made in Craftsman Fumed Oak. Seat and back of Craftsman hard leather only.

Height of back from floor, 36″
Height of seat " " 18″
Size of seat, 21″ wide, 19″ deep
Price, ... $21.00

OFFICE REVOLVING SCREW & SPRING CHAIR

Number 363

Made in Craftsman Fumed Oak. Seat and back of Craftsman hard leather only.

Height of back from seat, 19″
Size of seat, 21″ wide, 19″ deep

A double band of leather is suspended between the back posts, forming a comfortable as well as practical back.

Price, ... $23.00

81

OFFICE ARM CHAIR

Number 360

Made in Craftsman Fumed Oak.
Seat and back covered in Craftsman hard or soft leather.

Height of back from floor, 37″
Height of seat   "   "   19″
Size of seat, 21″ wide, 18″ deep

Price, ... $18.00

OFFICE REVOLVING SCREW & SPRING CHAIR

Number 361

Made in Craftsman Fumed Oak.
Seat covered in Craftsman hard or soft leather.

Height of back from seat,   19″
Size of seat, 21″ wide, 18″ deep

Price, ... $23.00

82

OFFICE REVOLVING SCREW & SPRING CHAIR

Number 362

Made in Craftsman Fumed Oak.
Seat and back covered in Craftsman hard or soft leather.

Height of back from seat, 15″
Size of seat,18″ wide, 17″ deep.

Price, ... $17.00

BILLIARD CHAIR

Number 312½B

Made in Craftsman Fumed Oak.
Seat covered in hard or soft leather.

Height of back from floor,   45″
  "   " seat   "   "   26″
Size of seat, 21″ wide, 19″ deep

Price, ... $13.50

83

B O O K   R A C K

Number 74

Made in Craftsman Fumed Oak. Especially desirable for reference books.

31″ high, 30″ wide, 10″ deep

Price, ... $6.00

84

C O S T U M E R

Number 52

Made in Craftsman Fumed Oak. 72″ high, 4 iron hooks. Simple and serviceable.

Price, ... $7.00

C O S T U M E R

Number 53

Made in Craftsman Fumed Oak. 72″ high, 14″ wide, 6 iron hooks. Good design and ample capacity.

Price, ... $12.00

85

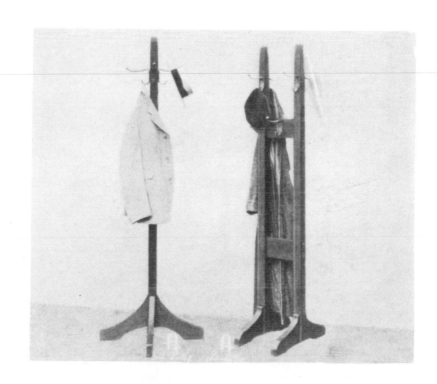

UMBRELLA STAND

Number 54

Made in Craftsman Fumed Oak. Removable copper pan. 29″ high, 12″ square

Price, ... $5.00

UMBRELLA STAND

Number 55

Made in Craftsman Fumed Oak. Three compartments. Removable copper pan.

29″ high, 21″ wide, 12″ deep

Price, ... $7.00

86

UMBRELLA   HOLDER

Number 80

Made in Craftsman Fumed Oak. Copper base, bands and removable pan. A practical piece.

27″ high, 12″ diameter

Price, ... $15.00

87

MAGAZINE CABINET

Number 72

Made in Craftsman Fumed Oak, Silver Gray Maple or Mahogany. A very useful piece of furniture in any room.

42″ high, 22″ wide, 13″ deep

Oak	Maple	Mahogany
$12.00	$13.25	$15.00

MAGAZINE CABINET

Number 79

Made in Craftsman Fumed Oak. A convenient rack for favorite books and periodicals.

40″ high, 14″ wide, 10″ deep

Price, ... $8,50

88

SMOKER'S CABINET

Number 78

Made in Craftsman Fumed Oak. Lock on door. Trimed in hand-wrought iron or copper.

29″ high, 20″ wide, 15″ deep

Price, ... $21.00

89

H A L L   M I R R O R

Number 66

Frame made in Craftsman Fumed Oak, 28″ x 36″. Best French plate mirror, 20″x30″. Iron hooks.

Price, ... $16.00

90

H A L L   M I R R O R

Number 67

Frame made in Craftsman Fumed Oak, 28″ x 42″. Two best French plate mirrors, 9″x20″; one 16″x20″. Four iron hooks. Very attractive hall-piece. May be placed above settle or bench.

Price, ... $18.75

91

HALL MIRROR

Number 68

Frame made in Craftsman Fumed Oak, 28″ x 48″. Two best French plate mirrors, 9″ x 20″; one 20″ x 20″. Four iron hooks.

Price, ... $21.00

92

THREE FOLD SCREEN

Number 81

Frame in Craftsman Fumed Oak, 58″ high, 54″ wide. Craftsman canvas in panels, appliqued with flower motifs. Colors of canvas and applique selected to harmonize with any color scheme.

Price, ... $20.00

93

THREE FOLD SCREEN

Number 82

Frame in Craftsman Fumed Oak. 72″ high; 67″ wide. Centre panel $26\frac{1}{2}$″ wide; side panels $20\frac{1}{4}$″ wide. Panels of Craftsman canvas appliqued with flower motifs, or of Craftsman leather,

Craftsman Canvas, . . $40.00
Craftsman Leather, . . 48.00

94

PLATE RACK

Number 801

Made in Craftsman Fumed Oak. Two grooved shelves. Designed to hang above No. 800 Sideboard.

28″ high, 48″ wide, 5″ deep

Price, ... $13.50

95

S I D E B O A R D

Number 800

Made in Craftsman Fumed Oak. Hand-wrought pulls in iron or copper. Top small drawers lined in ooze leather. Middle top and lower drawers equipped with good locks.

39″ high, 54″ wide, 21″ deep

Price, ... $51.00

96

S E R V I N G   T A B L E

Number 802

Made in Craftsman Fumed Oak. Two good-sized drawers with hand-wrought pulls in iron or copper.

36″ high, 42″ wide, 18″ deep

Price, ... $26.00

97

CHINA CABINET

Number 803

Made in Craftsman Fumed Oak, with clear glass panelled sides and door. Hand-wrought iron or copper pull and lock. Three adjustable shelves.

60″ high, 36″ wide, 15″ deep

Price, ... $38.00

98

SERVING TABLE

Number 808

Made in Craftsman Fumed Oak. Hand-wrought pulls in iron or copper. Top middle drawer lined in ooze leather. May be substituted for side-board.

40″ high, 48″ wide, 18″ deep

Price, ... $40.00

SERVING TABLE

Number 809

Made in Craftsman Fumed Oak. Design like No. 808 Serving Table.

40″ high, 54″ wide, 18″ deep

Price, ... $48.00

99

S I D E B O A R D

Number 804

Made in Craftsman Fumed Oak or Mahogany. Hand-wrought pulls in iron, copper or old brass. Top side drawers lined in ooze leather; two good-sized cupboards. Lower drawer deep and long enough to hold table-cloths.

42″ high, 54″ wide, 22″ deep

Oak	Mahogany
$85.00	$100.00

100

C H I N A   C A B I N E T

Number 815

Made in Craftsman Fumed Oak or Mahogany. Clear glass panes set in sash. Ample capacity. Adjustable shelves.

$65\frac{1}{2}″$ high, 40″ wide, 15″ deep

Oak	Mahogany
$48.00	$59.00

101

S I D E B O A R D

Number 814

Made in Craftsman Fumed Oak. Hand-wrought hinges and pulls in iron or copper. Top drawer lined in ooze leather. The plate rail is a useful feature.

48″ high, 60″ wide, 22″ deep

Price, ... $80.00

102

GONG AND STAND

Number 812

Made in Craftsman Fumed Oak. Solid copper gong of rich and mellow tone. The top is useful as a serving table.

36″ high, 31″ wide, 12″ deep

Price, ... $30.00

103

DINING TABLE

Number 632

Made in Craftsman Fumed Oak or Mahogany. This table is castored, and is designed for use in small rooms where lighter pieces are desired. Leaves made to match top. Lock for use when table is not extended.

48″ top—to extend 8 ft.	
Oak	Mahogany
$33.00	$41.50

48″ top—to extend 10 ft.	
Oak	Mahogany
$38.00	$47.50

54″ top—to extend 10 ft.	
Oak	Mahogany
$40.00	$48.00

54″ top—to extend 12 ft.	
Oak	Mahogany
$48.00	$57.00

104

DINING TABLE

Number 633

Made in Craftsman Fumed Oak. This table is castored, and is of the same design but larger size and heavier stock than No. 632. Leaves made and finished to match top. Lock for use when table is not extended.

54″ top—to extend 10 ft., $48.00

54″ "   "   "   12 "   58.00

60″ "   "   "   12 "   70.00

105

DINING TABLE

Number 634

Made in Craftsman Fumed Oak. This table is castored. The centre post is divided in halves enclosing movable leg, which supports table when extended. Leaves made and finished to match top. Lock for use when table is not extended.

54″ top—to extend	10 ft.,	$60.00
54″ " " "	12 "	70.00
60″ " " "	12 "	82.00

106

DINING TABLE

Number 631

Made in Craftsman Fumed Oak. Will easily seat twelve people. Of massive design, and adapted for use in a large room.

30″ high, 96″ long, 48″ wide

Price, ... $66.00

107

DINING CHAIR

Number 348½

Craftsman Fumed Oak or Mahogany. Craftsman leather seat. Height of back from floor, 31''; height of seat from floor, 14''; seat, 16'' x 16''.

Oak	Mahogany
$6.00	$7.50

ARM DINING CHAIR

Number 348½A

Craftsman Fumed Oak or Mahogany. Craftsman leather seat. Height of back from floor, 36''; height of seat from floor, 13''; seat, 20'' wide, 19'' deep.

Oak	Mahogany
$10.25	$12.75

DINING CHAIR

Number 348

Design and dimensions same as 348½. Rush or sheepskin seat.

Oak	Mahogany
$5.00	$6.25

ARM DINING CHAIR

Number 348A

Design and dimensions same as 348½A. Rush or sheepskin seat.

Oak	Mahogany
$8.75	$11.00

108

DINING CHAIR

Number 351

Craftsman Fumed Oak. Rush seat. Height of back from floor, 35''; height of seat from floor, 18''; seat, 16'' x 16''.

Price, ... $6.75

ARM DINING CHAIR

Number 351½A

Craftsman Fumed Oak. Seat in Craftsman leather. Height of back from floor, 37''; height of seat from floor, 19''; seat, 20'' wide, 19'' deep.

Price, ... $11.25

DINING CHAIR

Number 351½

Seat in Craftsman leather. Design and dimensions like No. 351.

Price, ... $7.75

ARM DINING CHAIR

Number 351A

Rush seat. Design and dimensions like No. 351½A.

Price, ... $9.75

109

DINING CHAIR

Number 352

Made in Craftsman Fumed Oak.
Slip seat in Craftsman leather or
rush.

Height of back from floor, 37″
Height of seat " " 18″
Size of seat, 16″ wide, 13″ deep

Price, ... $7.75

ARM DINING CHAIR

Number 352A

Made in Craftsman Fumed Oak.
Slip seat in Craftsman leather or
rush.

Height of back from floor, 40″
Height of seat " " 18″
Size of seat, 19″ wide, 16″ deep

Price, ... $11.00

110

DINING CHAIR

Number 349½

Made in Craftsman Fumed Oak.
Craftsman leather seat.

Height of back from floor, 38″
Height of seat " " 18″
Size of seat, 18″ wide, 17″ deep

Price, ... $7.50

ARM DINING CHAIR

Number 349½A

Made in Craftman Fumed Oak.
Craftsman leather seat.

Height of back from floor, 38″
Height of seat " " 18″
Size of seat, 22″ wide, 19″ deep

Price, ... $11.00

111

DINING CHAIR

Number 357

Made in Craftsman Fumed Oak. Seat in Craftsman hard leather, studded with dull brass or black nails.

Height of back from floor, 36"
Height of seat " " 18"
Size of seat, 18" wide, 16" deep

Price, ... $6.50

ARM DINING CHAIR

Number 357A

Made in Craftsman Fumed Oak. Seat in Craftsman hard leather, studded with dull brass or black nails.

Height of back from floor, 38"
Height of seat " " 18"
Size of seat, 17" wide, 15" deep

Price, ... $10.00

112

DINING CHAIR

Number 354½

Craftsman Fumed Oak or Mahogany. Seat in Craftsman leather. Height of back from floor, 36"; height of seat from floor, 18"; seat, 17" wide, 16" deep.

Oak $8.00   Mahogany $10.00

ARM DINING CHAIR

Number 354½A

Craftsman Fumed Oak or Mahogany. Seat in Craftsman leather. Height of back from floor, 36"; height of seat from floor, 17"; seat, 20" wide, 17" deep.

Oak $11.50   Mahogany $14.25

DINING CHAIR

Number 354

Rush or Sheepskin seat. Design and dimensions like No. 354½.

Oak, ... $7.00

ARM DINING CHAIR

Number 354A

Rush or Sheepskin seat. Design and dimensions like No. 354½A.

Oak, ... $10.00

113

DINING CHAIR

Number 353

Made in Craftsman Fumed Oak or Mahogany. Slip seat in Craftsman leather or rush. Light and serviceable.

Height of back from floor, 40"
Height of seat " " 18"
Size of seat, 15" wide, 14" deep

Oak	Mahogany
$7.75	$9.75

ARM DINING CHAIR

Number 353A

Made in Craftsman Fumed oak or Mahogany. Slip seat in Craftsman leather or rush.

Height of back from floor, 41"
Height of seat " " 18"
Size of seat, 18" wide, 16" deep

Oak	Mahogany
$10.75	$13.50

114

DINING CHAIR

Number 356

Made in Craftsman Fumed Oak. Seat and back covered in Craftsman hard or soft leather. Very heavy, lending dignity to a dining room.

Height of back from floor, 37"
Height of seat " " 19"
Size of seat, 19" wide, 18" deep

Price, ... $16.00

ARM DINING CHAIR

Number 356A

Made in Craftsman Fumed Oak. Seat and back covered in Craftsman hard or soft leather.

Height of back from floor, 39"
Height of seat " " 19"
Size of seat, 23" wide, 22" deep

Price, ... $22.00

115

DINING CHAIR
Number 355

Made in Craftsman Fumed Oak. Seat and back covered in Craftsman hard leather. A very heavy chair, adapted for use in a large room.

Height of back from floor, 35″
Height of seat " " 19″
Size of seat, 19″ wide, 17″ deep

Price, ... $20.00

ARM DINING CHAIR
Number 355A

Made in Craftsman Fumed Oak. Seat and back covered in Craftsman hard leather.

Height of back from floor, 37″
Height of seat " " 19″
Size of seat, 23″ wide, 21″ deep

Price, ... $26.00

116

STAND
Number 641

Made in Craftsman Fumed Oak, Silver Gray Maple or Mahogany. Wooden drawer pulls. This stand is designed especially for bedrooms.

29″ high; top, 17½″ x 20″

Oak	Maple	Mahogany
$10.00	$11.00	$12.50

SMALL CHAIR
Number 338
Matches No. 337 Rocker

Height of back from floor, 40″
Height of seat " " 18″
Size of seat, 15″ wide, 14″ deep

Oak	Maple	Mahogany
$7.75	$8.50	$9.75

117

DRESSING TABLE

Number 914

Made in Craftsman Fumed Oak, Silver Gray Maple or Mahogany. Wood, or hand-wrought pulls in iron, copper or old brass.

Height from floor to top of mirror, $55\frac{1}{2}''$

Height from floor to top of table, 30''

Size of top, 36'' wide, 18'' deep

Best French Plate Glass, 20'' x 24''

Oak	Maple	Mahogany
$26.00	$28.50	$31.50

118

DRESSER

Number 915

Made in Craftsman Fumed Oak, Silver Gray Maple or Mahogany.

Height of top from floor, 33''
Size of top, 42'' x 20''
Height of cabinet from top, 9''
Size of cabinet top, 34'' x $8\frac{1}{2}''$

Oak	Maple	Mahogany
$47.00	$51.75	$57.00

MIRROR

Number 916

FOR No. 915 DRESSER

Made in Craftsman Fumed Oak, Silver Gray Maple or Mahogany. Frame 30'' wide, 24'' high. Best French plate mirror.

Oak	Maple	Mahogany
$12.50	$13.25	$14.75

119

D R E S S E R

Number 911

Made in Craftsman Fumed Oak, Silver Gray Maple or Mahogany. Wood, or hand-wrought pulls in iron, copper or old brass.

Height from floor to top of mirror, 66″

Height from floor to top of case, 33″

Size of top, 48″ wide, 22″ deep

Best French Plate Glass, 28″ x 34″

Oak	Maple	Mahogany
$50.00	$55.00	$60.00

120

CHEST OF DRAWERS

Number 913

Made in Craftsman Fumed Oak, Silver Gray Maple or Mahogany, with panelled sides. Three large, six small drawers, with dust-proof partitions. Wood, or hand-wrought pulls in iron, copper or old brass.

$50\frac{1}{2}$″ high, 36″ wide, 20″ deep

Oak	Maple	Mahogany
$39.00	$43.00	$48.75

121

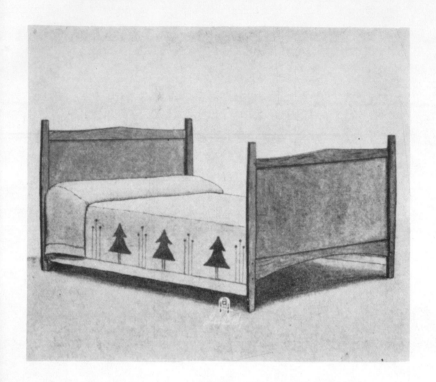

BEDSTEAD

Number 912

Made in Craftsman Fumed Oak, Silver Gray Maple or Mahogany. The natural beauty of the wood is well-displayed in head and foot board.

4' 6" wide, 6' 3" long, (inside measurements).

Head, 4' 3" high; foot, 3' 9"

Oak	Maple	Mahogany
$30.00	$33.00	$37.50

122

CHEVAL GLASS

Number 918

Made in Craftsman Fumed Oak, Silver Gray Maple or Mahogany. Best French plate mirror.

Frame, 70" high; 34" wide.

Glass, 22" x 54"

Oak	Maple	Mahogany
$35.00	$38.50	$40.00

123

CHEST OF DRAWERS

Number 902

Made in Craftsman Fumed Oak, with panelled sides. Hand-wrought pulls in iron or copper. Dust-proof partitions between drawers. Four commodious drawers, two small ones.

50″ high, 40″ wide, 22″ deep

Price, ... $60.00

124

CHEST OF DRAWERS

Number 901

Made in Craftsman Fumed Oak, with panelled sides. Hand-wrought pulls in iron or copper. Dust-proof partitions between drawers. Ample drawer room.

40″ high, 36″ wide, 20″ deep

Price, ... $40.00

125

D R E S S E R

Number 903

Made in Craftsman Fumed Oak, with panelled sides. Hand-wrought pulls in iron or copper. Large drawers separated by dust-proof partitions.

33″ high, 54″ wide, 22″ deep

Price, ... $62.00

M I R R O R

Number 904

For No. 903 Dresser. Frame made in Craftsman Fumed Oak, 32″ x 54″. Best French Plate Glass, 26″ x 48″. Hand-wrought sconces at side, in iron, copper or old brass.

Price, ... $36.00

126

B E D S T E A D

Number 917

Made in Craftsman Fumed Oak. 4′ 6″ wide, 6′ 3″ long, (inside measurements). Head, 4′ 6″ high; foot, 3′ 7″ high.

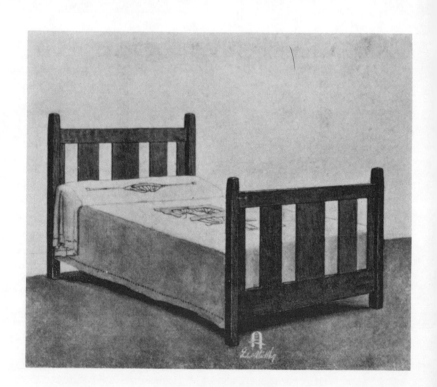

Price, ... $32.00

127

DESCRIPTION OF THE WOOD FINISHING METHODS OF GUSTAV STICKLEY

Over the last seventy years, Arts and Crafts furniture has suffered much abuse and it is seldom, indeed, that one has the opportunity to study a piece in its original state. Even examples which exist in good condition remain so because they have been subjected to years of loving polishing which of course has changed the appearance of the unfilled wood grain. Stickley's most innovative work was in wood finish. His attempts to recreate "weathered oak" were a departure from the standard methods of wood finishing. The green finish, of which he was particularly proud, evidently faded quickly and the dull silvered maple is seldom seen today so one must rely on written descriptions of finishes Stickley formulated.

The cabinet work which first brought Mr. Gustav Stickley into prominence is distinguished by a marked style and finish. It is made from oak and other native woods, with the use of the former greatly predominating. The finish is quickly recognized by those who have once examined it, and, particularly as it appears in the "fumed oak," it is acknowledged by competent judges as unparalleled. It gives to the wood the look of age, without injuring its natural qualities: preserving, or rather enhancing the beauties of grain, and accentuating the "watered," pattern-like effects which run through its texture. The finish, produced by the use of chemical agents, does not create a surface gathering dust and impurities and finally making the object which it coats ugly to the eye and harsh to the touch. It acts rather as a protection to the substance of the wood against wear and exposure. Its two most successful applications are in a mellow, deep-toned brown, and a soft brown-gray.

In The Craftsman Workshops, the treatment of wood is matched by the manner of dressing leather. In this substance, also, the signs manual of Nature are preserved: the cross-hatchings, the *papillae,* the softness and pliability; so that when the skin is completely dressed, it yields to the touch, and appears to the eye almost as if it were still fed by the life of the animal. The colors as well as the finish given to the leather, are designed to match the woods, to the end that both materials, together with the textiles, may concur in a general decorative scheme. Again, in the leathers, the most successful experiments are in gamuts of browns, greens and grays. With these must be mentioned also certain iridescent qualities equaling in beauty the "watered" or *moiré* effects occurring in the best examples of the "fumed oak."

FINISHING WOOD FOR PROTECTION AND HARMONY

In finishing wood two chief aims must be kept in mind: protection of its surface from damp and soil, and attainment of such color and texture as will bring the wood into harmony with its surroundings. Naturally the method of obtaining these results varies according to the kind of wood and the effect desired.

Until a few years ago the finishing of our native woods was confined almost entirely to the staining of the cheaper woods to imitate the more expensive ones. For instance, when walnut was in vogue, the less costly woods were stained to look like walnut; when mahogany was deemed the most fashionable, they were colored to imitate mahogany. And it is only within a comparatively recent period that we have begun to realize that the most beautiful results are those attained by bringing out the inherent characteristics of each kind of wood, letting the peculiarities and qualities of the wood itself suggest the most appropriate treatment.

The natural tones of our native woods, with few exceptions—notably black walnut—are not strong enough to harmonize with the furnishings of the average interior,

117

and therefore the original color of most woods must be deepened when used for furniture, floors and interior trim. Besides, even when the wood has some color of its own, it will often fade unless deepened artificially, as in the case of birch, which has a rich reddish tone but fades when exposed to light. Moreover, the raw wood lacks that mellowness which Nature always gives by her healing and weathering processes to any exposed surface, and needs some treatment which will supply this lack and bring it into harmony with an interior.

COLORS MOST APPROPRIATE FOR WOODWORK

Working along the lines suggested above, it naturally seems best, in coloring wood, to give to it by art such colors, on the whole, as might have been given by Nature. There are many rich browns, for instance, that resemble the colors in the bark of the tree; mellow greenish stains suggest that moss-grown trunk and colors of the foliage, while soft shades of brownish gray recall the hues produced by weathering. Thus the choice is somewhat limited, brown, green and brownish gray, with their different shades and variations, being the only colors that can be appropriately used.

BEST METHOD OF FINISHING OAK

The work of construction must all be done before the wood is given its final finish; but in this connection we will outline briefly the best method of finishing oak, as the sturdy wooden quality of the furniture depends entirely upon the ability of the worker to treat the wood so that there is little evidence of an applied finish. Oak should be ripened as the old mahogany was ripened by oil and sunshine, and this can be done only by a process that, without altering or disguising the nature of the wood, gives it the appearance of having been mellowed by age and use. This process is merely fuming with ammonia, which has a certain affinity with the tannic acid that exists in the wood, and it is the only one known to us that acts upon the glossy hard rays as well as the softer parts of the wood, coloring all together in an even tone so that the figure is marked only by its difference in texture. This result is not so good when stains are used instead of fuming, as staining leaves the soft part of the wood dark and the markings light and prominent.

FUMING WITH AMMONIA

The fuming is not an especially difficult process, but it requires a good deal of care, for the piece must be put into an air-tight box or closet, on the floor of which has been placed shallow dishes containing aqua ammonia (26 per cent). The length of time required to fume oak to a good color depends largely upon the tightness of the compartment, but as a rule forty-eight hours is enough. When fuming is not practicable, as in the case of a piece too large for any available compartment or one that is built into the room, a fairly good result may be obtained by applying the strong ammonia directly to the wood with a sponge or brush. In either case the wood must be in its natural condition when treated, as any previous application of oil or stain would keep the ammonia from taking effect. After the wood so treated is thoroughly dry from the first application it should be sandpapered carefully with fine sandpaper, then a second coat of ammonia applied, followed by a second careful sandpapering.

"TOUCH-UP" TO EVEN COLOR AND FINAL FINISHING

Some pieces fume much darker than others, according to the amount of tannin left free to attract the ammonia after the wood has been kiln-dried. Where any sap wood has been left on, that part will be found unaffected by the fumes. There is apt also to be a slight difference in tone when the piece is not all made from the same log, because some trees contain more tannic acid than others. To meet these conditions it is necessary to make a "touch-up" to even the color. This is done by mixing a brown aniline dye (that will dissolve in alcohol) with German lacquer, commonly known as "banana liquid," [probably amyl acetate]. The mixture may be thinned with wood alcohol to the right consistency before using. In touching up the lighter portions of the wood the stain may be smoothly blended with the darker tint of the perfectly fumed parts, by rubbing along the line where they join with a piece of soft dry cheese-cloth, closely following the brush. If the stain should dry too fast and the color is left uneven, dampen the cloth very slightly with alcohol. After fuming, sandpapering and touching up a piece of furniture, apply a coat of lacquer, made of one-third white shellac and two-thirds German lacquer. If the fuming process has resulted in a shade dark enough to be satisfactory, this lacquer may be applied clear; if not, it may be darkened by the addition of a small quantity of the stain used in touching up. Care must be taken, however, to carry on the color so lightly that it will not grow muddy under the brush of an inexperienced worker. The danger of this makes it often more advisable to apply two coats of lacquer, each containing a very little color. If this is done, sandpaper each coat with very fine sandpaper after it is thoroughly dried and then apply one or more coats of prepared floor wax. These directions, if carefully followed, should give the same effects that characterize the Craftsman furniture.

HOW TO OBTAIN A BROWNISH-GRAY FINISH

The gray finish can be obtained by brushing onto the wood a weak solution of iron rust. This can be made either by throwing iron filings, rusty nails or any small pieces of iron into acid vinegar or acetic acid, and after a couple of days straining off the solution and diluting it with water until it is of the strength needed to get the desired color on the wood. Or if preferred, a solution of chloride of iron and water may be used instead of the vinegar and iron rust. In either case, it is absolutely essential to experiment first with small pieces of wood, to judge as to the strength of the solution needed to give the desired effect. The color does not show at all until dry.

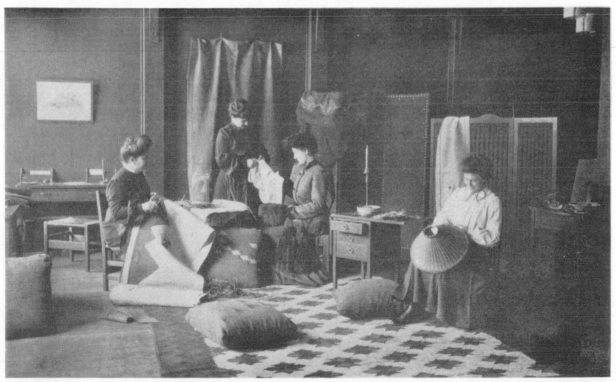

NEEDLEWORKERS   Craftsman Building

RETAIL PLATES PUBLISHED BY GUSTAV STICKLEY

Gustav Stickley sold some of his furniture directly from the factory by catalogue. However, the greater portion was distributed through the more than fifty retail establishments in major cities across the United States and Canada. These "associates" obviously could not carry examples of each piece of furniture from Stickley's extensive designs and so they were given special salesmen's catalogues to help supplement their own stock. The following plates are an example of this type of merchandising technique.

88   206   88   220

89   210   89   392   336   332

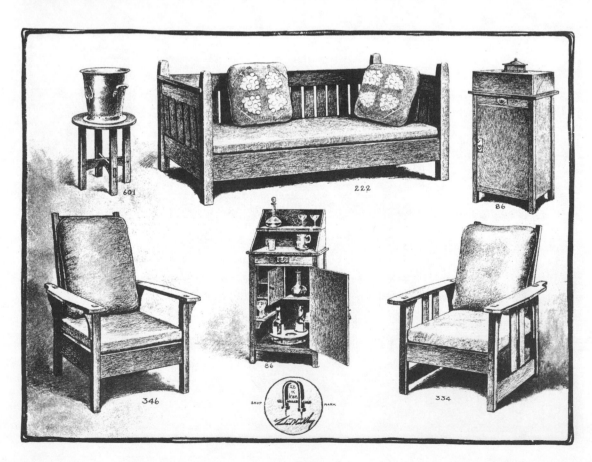

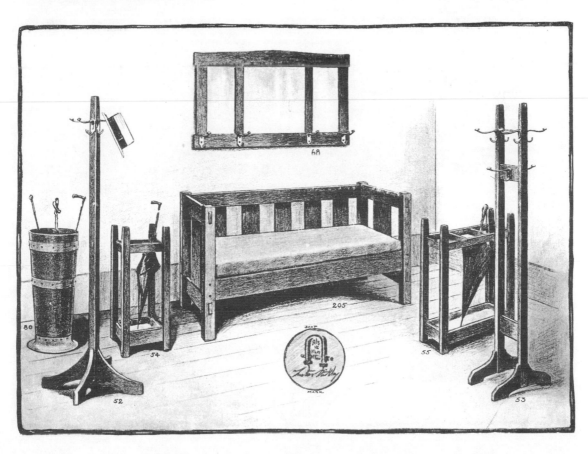

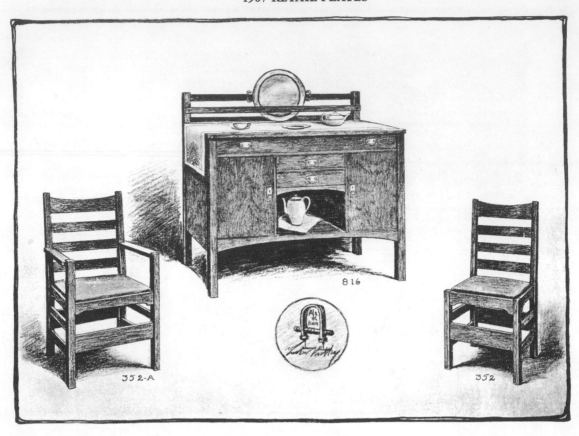

816

352-A

352

814

818

356

356A

817

354-A

354

808

804

815

354½

634

354½A

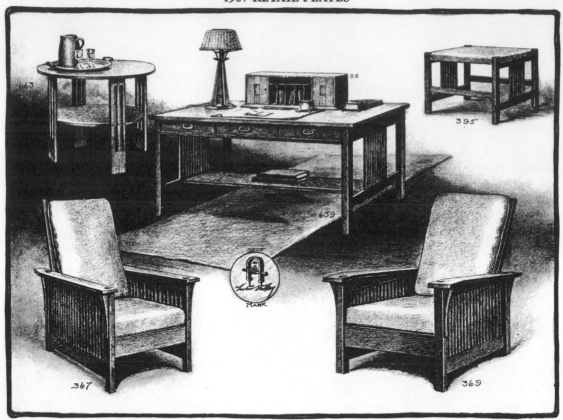

358   654   98   358 A

359   630   359 A

819   629   820

358 A   358

310

309

651

309½

310½

627

656

370

370 A

349½ A

349½

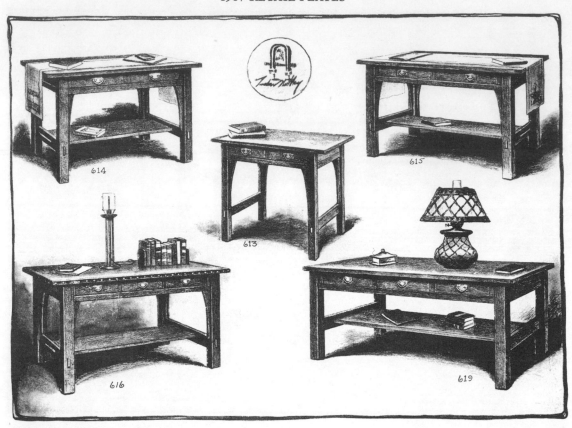

614

615

613

616

619

72

645

79

652

653

637

635

625

636

607

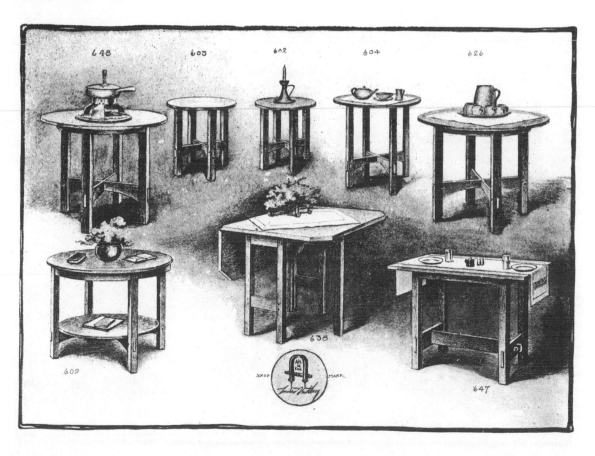

648   605   602   604   626

638

609

647

715

SHOP MARK

717

612

716½

660

701½

703

700

74

SHOP MARK

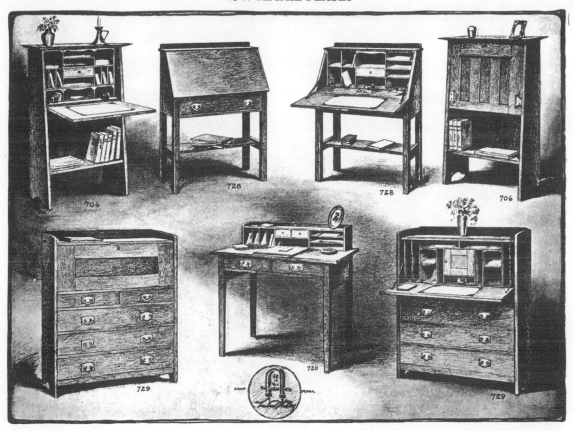

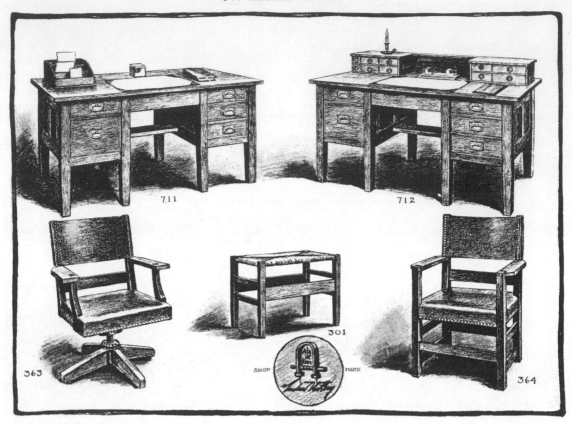

LEATHER WORKERS

Craftsman Workshops, Eastwood, N. Y.

METAL WORKERS

Craftsman Building

HAND-WROUGHT METAL WORK FROM THE CRAFTSMAN WORKSHOPS, circa 1905

Metal work came into the Craftsman inventory as a result of Stickley's dissatisfaction with the hardware commercially available for use in his cabinet work. Bail handles, strap hinges and fireplace equipment were made at the workshop but the popular fascination for "Russian" brass and copper led him to such far flung sources as England and Germany for many of the accessories which were offered in later catalogues.

Old European metal work is highly prized by all persons of artistic tastes, who recognize in the object wrought the enthusiasm of the workman who wrought it. Every piece of this hammered copper, brass, or iron, bears, as it were, a signature, stamped in its form, and in its individual manner of treatment. It is strong enough to recall to the mind of the examiner a picture of the mediæval workshop with its picturesqueness and its ceaseless activity.

The spirit animating the old system of labor, is fostered in the Craftsman Workshops, where the artisans in many cases, can trace a long ancestry of toil; their forefathers having for generations exercised the same trade in a single city, village, or hamlet of the old world. For this reason, they pursue their work, as naturally as they follow the routine of their physical life, or as cheerfully as they use their language.

Their leader is a type of his species in both person and capacity; working to-day with the spirit and the extreme diligence which were characteristic of the times when the handicrafts were cultivated as a religion. Projected against the firelight of the flaming forge, his sinewy frame satisfies the spectator with a sense of fitness, as he moves with quick, decisive gesture, directing the processes of the men who are shaping a large number of objects, widely differing in size and use: such as Lamps, Lanterns, Electroliers, Candlesticks, Umbrella Stands, Jardinieres, Wine Coolers, Cigar Boxes, Serving Trays, Wall Plaques, Hinges, Drawer Pulls, Knockers and Escutcheons.

Of these the present booklet offers a certain number of the more usual examples. But the same workmen produce all kinds of architectural and decorative iron work: such as Fire-place Hoods, Andirons of unique design, Hinges and Door Latches, Window Gratings, Gateways, and Doors: these being executed, at the will of the patron, according to schemes furnished by him, or after designs produced in the Craftsman Workshops.

Every article of this metal work is made with the utmost care; the iron receiving the finish known in England as "armor bright," which offers a soft, pleasing surface effect; while the objects in brass and copper are subjected to an old process of firing, which develops a richness of texture not obtainable by any other method. It may further be said that no laquer is used on copper or brass; age and exposure being the only agents, excepting the unique finish, required to produce beauty and variety of tone.

349

Andirons

Wrought iron.   Height, 33″; depth, 30″

348

Andirons

Wrought iron.   Height, 28″; depth, 26″

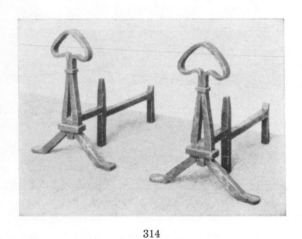

314

Andirons

Wrought iron.   Height, 18″; depth, 22″

88

Andirons

Wrought iron.   Height, 20″; depth, 21″

237

Andirons

Wrought iron.   Height, 24″; depth, 21″

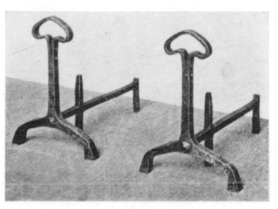

315

Andirons

Wrought iron.   Height, 16½″; depth, 20″

102

Andirons

Wrought iron.   Height, 21″; depth, 21″

350

Coal Bucket

Hammered copper or brass, wrought iron trimmings
Height of bucket, 15″

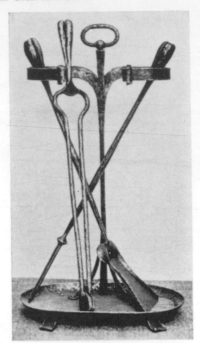

138

Fire Set

Wrought iron. Shovel No. 206, length, 30″; Poker
No. 207, length, 30″; Tongs No. 208, length, 30″
Standard No. 137, length, 29″

351

Coal Bucket

Hammered copper or brass, wrought iron handles
Height, 16″.   Diameter of base, 11½″

Art Glass Lamp Shades

In the accompanying pages are shown several designs of <u>Art Glass Lamp Shades</u>. These shades are especially designed with a view of a perfect and harmonious effect in their use with our special hammered copper oil lamps. The frames of the shades are finished in copper to match the rich effect of the hammered copper bases of the lamps. The glass used is selected for its beautiful color effect when shown with the light of the burner. The colors selected are also those best adapted to use with prevailing tones of decorations. All glass is leaded and the shades are finished in the best manner possible.

No. 650.   Yellow opalescent glass in body of shade with green and red in band.   16″ in diameter.

No. 651.   Green opalescent glass in body of shade with two shades of red in band.   16″ in diameter.

No. 652.   Ruby glass in body of shade with green in band. 16″ in diameter.

No. 653.   Yellow opalescent glass in body of shade with green in the three bands.   14″ in diameter.

No. 654.   Green opalescent glass in body of shade with Ruby in the three bands.   14″ in diameter.

No. 655.   Ruby opalescent glass in body of shade with green in the three bands.   14″ in diameter.

No. 662.   Green opalescent glass panels.   14″ in diameter.

No. 663.   Ruby glass panels.   14″ in diameter.

No. 664.   Yellow opalescent glass panels.   14″ in diameter.

No.   5.   Glass Mosaic varying shade in greens.   12″ in diameter at base.

No. 666.   Copper Shade in stencil pattern, with wire gauze back and brass fringe.   Straight Line Motif.

No. 667.   Copper Shade, in stencil pattern with wire gauze backing and brass fringe.   Bird Motif.

No. 668.   Copper Shade, in stencil pattern with wire gauze backing and brass fringe.   Flower Motif.

293

Oil Lamp

Base and Fount in copper.   Handles in wrought iron.   Height
to top of burner, 14″   Shade Nos. 653, 654 or 655

Oil Lamp

Fount in copper, with wrought iron standard.   Japanese wic
shade.   Made of wicker, enameled a rich, dark browr
Lining of plaited silk in green or dull red.   Diameter
at bottom of shade, 17½″; Height, 7¼″; opening at
top, 5¼″.   Shade, No. 669.   Lamp, No. 376.

295

Oil Lamp

Base and Fount in copper.   Handles in wrought iron.   Height
to top of burner, 14″.   Shade Nos. 662, 663 or 664.

294

Oil Lamp

Base and Fount in copper.   Handles in wrought iron.   Heigh
to top of burner, 16″.   Shade Nos. 650, 651 or 652.

320

Oil Lamp

ase and Fount in copper.   Height to top of burner, 21″
Shade Nos. 650, 651 or 652.

319

Oil Lamp

Base and Fount in hammered copper.   Height to top of burner
21½″   Shade Nos. 650, 651 or 652.

203

Electric Lantern

Wrought iron or hammered copper.   Chain and ceiling
plate in wrought iron.   Globe in amber tinted
hammered glass.   Height, 20″;
Base, 13½″ x 13½″

322

Oil Lamp

Base and Fount in copper.   Height to top of burner, 18″
Shade Nos. 650, 651 or 652.

380
Oil Lamp

Fount in copper, with standard of wrought iron. Height to top of burner 15″. Shade No. 5. Glass Mosaic varying shades in greens. 12″ in diameter.

376
Oil Lamp

Fount in copper, with wrought iron standard. Shade No. 66? Copper in stencil pattern with backing of brass gauze. Brass linked fringe.

202
Electric Lantern

Wrought iron, hammered copper or brass, with chain socket and fixtures wire for hanging. Height, 8″. 3″ opalescent, crystal, and amber globe.

204
Electric Lantern

Wrought iron, hammered copper or brass. 6″ yellow opalescent globe. Height of lantern, 12″

205

Electric Lantern

Wrought iron, hammered copper or brass, with chain
socket and fixture wire for hanging   Height,
8"; 3" opalescent, crystal or amber globe

202½

Electric Lantern

Wrought iron, hammered copper or brass. Chain and ceiling
plate in wrought iron. Globe in yellow opalescent
glass. Chain socket.   Height, 14"; diameter of globe, 6"

205½

Electric Lantern

Wrought iron, hammered copper or brass. Chain and ceiling
plate in wrought iron. Chain socket. Globe in
amber tinted hammered glass. Height,
13"; top of lantern, 11"

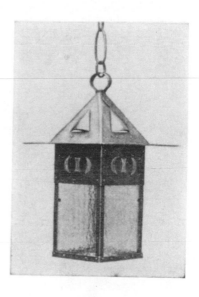

324

Electric Lantern

Wrought iron, hammered copper or brass. Chain and ceiling
plate in wrought iron. Globe in yellow opalescent
glass. Chain socket. Height, 14"; diameter of globe, 6"

323

Electric Lantern with Bracket

Wrought iron, hammered copper or brass. Chain and bracket in wrought iron. Lantern 13″ high, with amber tinted hammered glass. Chain socket. Projection of bracket 9″

31

225

Electric Lantern with Bracket

Lantern wrought iron, hammered copper or brass
Height, 8″. 3″ opalescent, crystal, or amber globe.
Bracket in wrought iron only. Height, 7″; projection, 5¼″

32

400

Electric Fixture and Bracket

Bell-shape Globe, size 5½″ x 3″; height of Bracket, 10″; Projection, 8″. In opalescent, crystal, and amber glass. Also made in 8″ x 4″. Bell-shape globe. Height of bracket, 12″. Projection, 9″. With or without bracket.

No. 402 Bell 5½″ x 3″ with chain and canopy
"   403   "   8″ x 4″   "   "   "   "
"   404   "   8″ x 4″   "   "   "   "

34

355

Electric Lantern with Bracket

Wrought iron, hammered copper or brass. Lantern 8″ high
with 3″ opalescent, crystal or amber globe.
Bracket, 21″ high; projection, 8″

33

277

Three Light Electrolier

Wrought iron, hammered copper or brass. Chain and ceiling plate in wrought iron.   Globes in opalescent, crystal and amber glass.   Diameter of ring, 12″; height of lanterns, 8″; diameter of globe, 3″

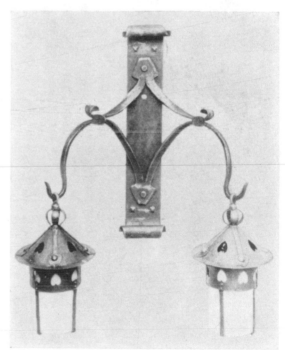

224

Two Light Electric Bracket Fixture

Lanterns in wrought iron, hammered copper or brass. Globes 3″ opalescent, crystal and amber glass.   Bracket in wrought iron.   Height of lantern, 8″; height of bracket, 14″

223½

Nine Light Electrolier

Wrought iron, hammered copper or brass. Chain and ceiling
plate in wrought iron.   Globe in opalescent, crystal and
amber glass   Diameter of ring, 24″; Height of lanterns,
8″; Diameter of globe, 3″

223

Five Light Electrolier

Wrought iron, hammered copper or brass. Chain and ceiling
plate in wrought iron.   Globes in opalescent, crystal and
amber glass.   Diameter of ring, 16″; height of lanterns,
8″; Diameter of globe 3″

304 **Four Light Electrolier**

nterns and Cross Bars in wrought iron or copper.   Wrought
iron chain.   Globes in amber tinted, hammered glass.
Length of Cross Bars 22″   Height of Lanterns, 11″

40

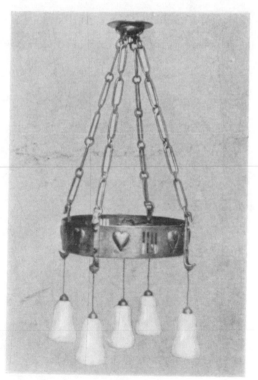

401

Electrolier

Five-light Electrolier, band of copper, iron chain, copper canopy,
bell shape.   Globes in opalescent, crystal, and amber.
Size of bell 5½″ x 3″.

39

359

Electric Candlestick

Cast brass, glass candle. 88″ silk lamp cord with socket. Height, 16″

262

Portable Electric Lamp

Wrought iron or hammered copper. Shade in ruby or yell opalescent glass. Switch and three chain sockets. Height, 23″; diameter of shade 16″

296

Candle Chandelier

Wrought iron, hammered copper or brass
Diameter of ring, 24″

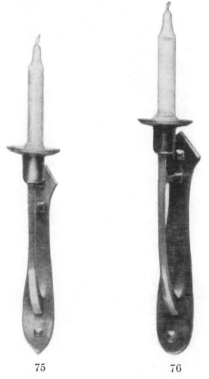

358

Candlestick

In cast brass.   Height, 8½″

75   76

Candle Brackets

Brass or copper.   Height of No. 75, 9″
Height of No. 76, 10¼″

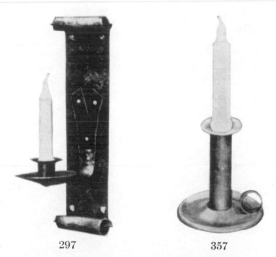

297   357

Candle Sconce and Candlestick

297.   Hammered brass or copper.   Height, 13″; width, 3″
357.   Brass.   Height, 4″

273

Umbrella Holder

Hammered copper.   Height, 27″
Diameter at top, 12″

382

Umbrella Stand

Hand wrought copper.   Height, 24″; diameter of top, 13″.

275

Jardiniere

Hammered copper.   Height 19″
Diameter at top, 12″

276

Jardiniere

Hammered copper.   Height, 12″
Diameter at top, 12″

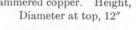

366

Cuspidor

Hammered Copper.   Base 10″.

268

Cigar Box

Hammered copper, interior in Spanish cedar.
Size: 5½″ x 7½″; 2½″ high.

308   299

Fern Holder

No. 308, body in hammered copper, legs in wrought iron.
Diameter, 7″
No. 299, body in hammered copper or wrought iron, legs in
wrought iron.   Diameter 9″.   Basin in terra cotta.

342

Cigar Box

Hammered copper, interior in Spanish cedar
Size: 7 x 11″, 6″ high

269   270

271   272

Ash Trays

Hammered copper.   Diameter of Nos. 272 and 269, 5¼″
Diameter of Nos. 271 and 270, 6¾″

298

Wine Cooler

Hammered copper. Height, 12″
Length at top, 18″, width at top, 8½″

352

Chafing Dish

Standard of hammered copper, on wood base, terra cotta
casserole.

346

Serving Tray

Hammered copper. Diameter, 20″

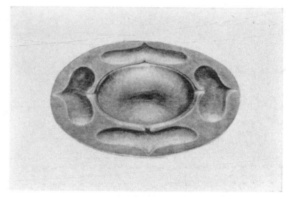

344

Wall Placque

Hammered copper. Diameter, 15″

347

Serving Tray

Hammered copper. Diameter, 20″

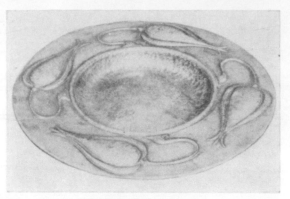

345

Wall Placque

Hammered copper.   Diameter, 20″

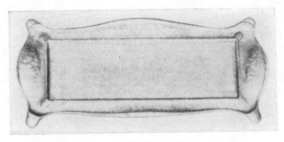

354

Serving Tray

Hammered copper.   Size, 10″ x 24″

274

Serving Tray

Hammered copper or brass.   Diameter 16″

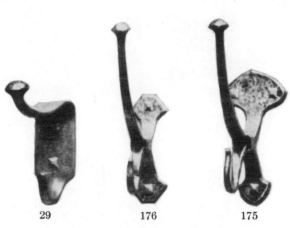

29   176   175

Hat and Coat Hooks

Wrought iron or hammered copper

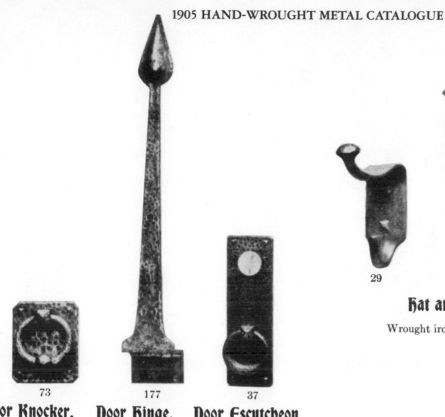

73   177   37

Door Knocker.   Door Hinge.   Door Escutcheon.

No. 73, Door Knocker, wrought iron. Size, 5″ x 6″
No. 177, Door Hinge, wrought iron. Size, 26″ long 4″ butt.
No. 37, Door Escutcheon, wrought iron (made for Yale lock),
      ring turns latch. Size, 3″ x 11″

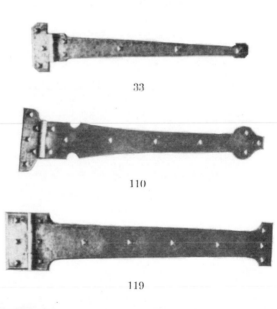

33

110

119

162

Hinges

Wrought iron or hammered copper

No. 33.   Length, 15½″; width of hinge back, 3½″
" 110.   "   17½″   "   "   "   "   4¾″
" 119.   "   19″   "   "   "   "   4″
" 162.   "   19½″   "   "   "   "   2⅜″

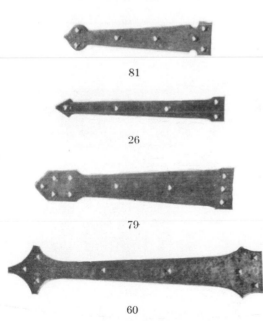

81

26

79

60

Hinge Plates

Wrought iron or hammered copper

No. 81.   Length, 11″.   For a 2½″ butt-
" 26.   "   12½″.   "   2″   "
" 79.   "   14″.   "   3″   "
" 60.   "   18½″.   "   3¼″   "

23   44   59

27   54   34

Drawer and Door Pulls

Wrought iron or hammered copper

Size, No. 27, $1\frac{5}{8}''$ x $4''$ Size, No. 44, $1\frac{1}{2}''$
"   "   54, $1\frac{3}{4}''$ x $4\frac{1}{4}''$ "   "   23, $3''$ x $3''$
"   "   34, $2\frac{1}{4}''$ x $5\frac{1}{8}''$ "   "   59, $2\frac{1}{4}''$ x $4\frac{1}{4}''$

38   171

24   134

31   118

Drawer Pulls

Wrought iron or hammered copper

Size, No. 38, $1\frac{1}{2}''$ x $3\frac{1}{4}''$ Size, No. 171, $2''$ x $4\frac{1}{4}''$
"   "   24, $2\frac{1}{8}''$ x $3\frac{3}{4}''$ "   "   134, $2\frac{3}{8}''$ x $5''$
"   "   31, $2\frac{1}{4}''$ x $4\frac{1}{8}''$ "   "   118, $2\frac{7}{8}''$ x $5\frac{1}{2}''$

267

Door Pull and Escutcheon

Wrought iron or hammered copper
267.   Size, 1½″ x 4″

111   30

Small Hinges

Wrought iron or hammered copper.
No. 111, Size, 2¾″ x 3″
No. 30, Size, 2½″ x 4″

28   32

Key Escutcheons

Wrought iron or hammered copper.
No. 28, Size, ⅞″ x 3″.   No. 32, Size, 1¼″ x 3¼″

18   98

Drawer Pulls

Wrought iron or hammered copper
No 18, Size, ¾″ x 3⅜″.   No. 98, Size, ⅞″ x 5″

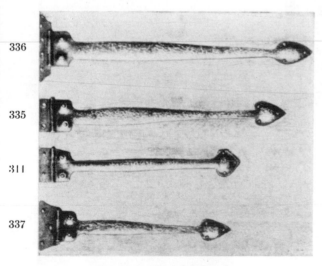

336

335

311

337

Wrought Iron Hinges

336.   Length, 16″; butt, 4⅛″
335.   Length, 14″; butt, 2″
311.   Length, 11″; butt, 2″
337.   Length, 10⅛″; butt, 3″

301

266

300

Drawer Pulls

Wrought iron, hammered copper or brass.
301.   Size, 1¾″ x 3¼″
266.   Size, 2″ x 4″
300.   Size, 2½″ x 4¼″

The Craftsman Tag

**Attached to all Articles made
in the Craftsman Workshops**

CONCLUSION

As the revival of interest in the American Arts and Crafts Movement gains momentum, its acceptance as an important period in decorative arts history will develop. Consequently, the furniture of Gustav Stickley will find its way into the marketplace in greater numbers as more people learn and appreciate its timeless-ness. Stickley's sturdy, rectilinear forms, emphasis on rich wood grain and lack of embellishment integrate well into contemporary settings. Catalogues such as this should help simplify the task of sorting through the many thousands of pieces that still exist in the possession of collectors and dealers and as heirlooms. Individuals who value rarity may begin to determine how long a design was in production at the factory; those who value aesthetics may compare all the possible variations of a particular form and those who value Stickley's ideas and philosophy may better understand how the cultural fabric of America was patterned at the turn of the century.

Stephen Gray
November, 1981